THIS COLORING BOOK BELONGS TO:

Color Chart

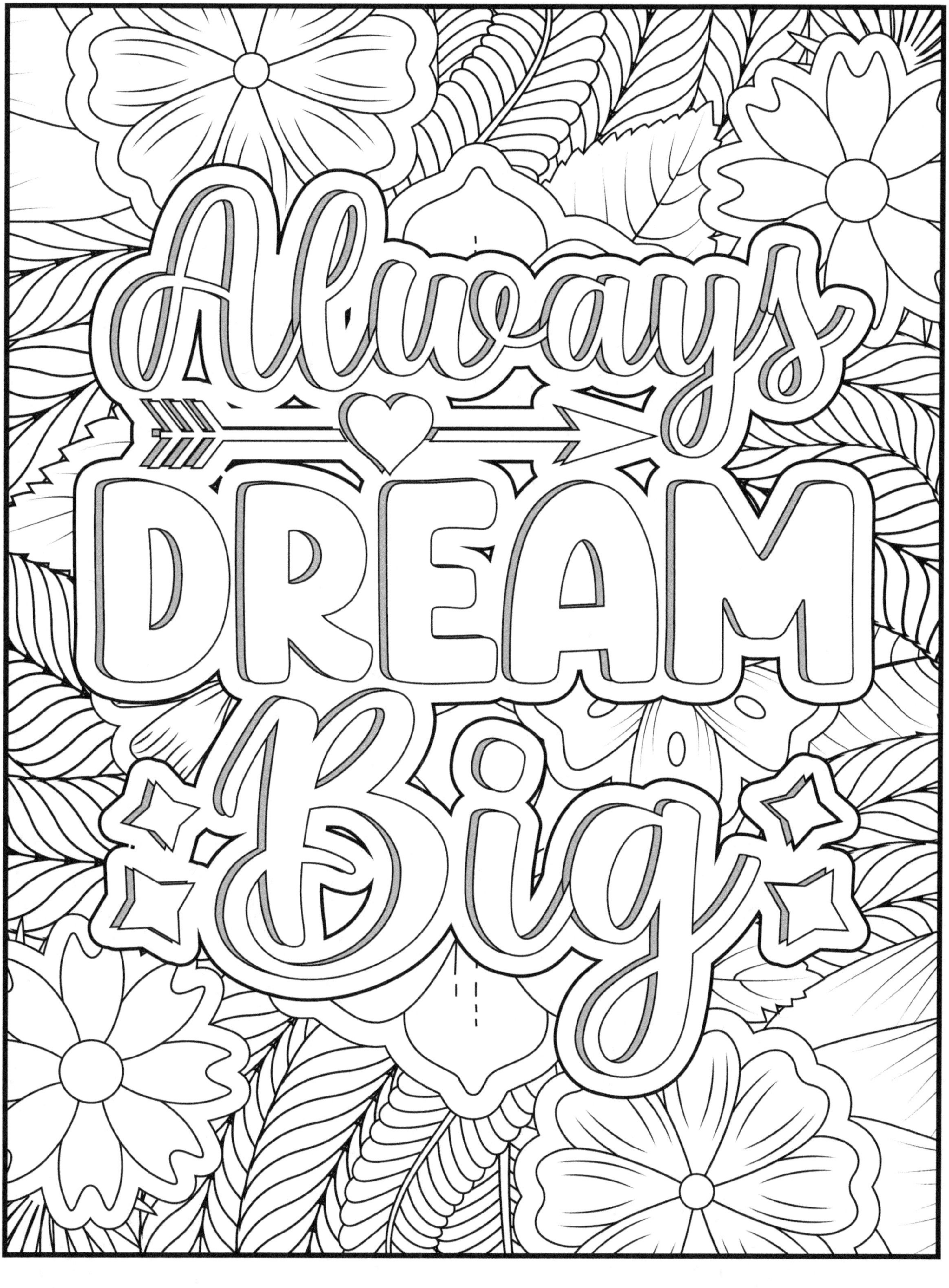
Always
DREAM
Big

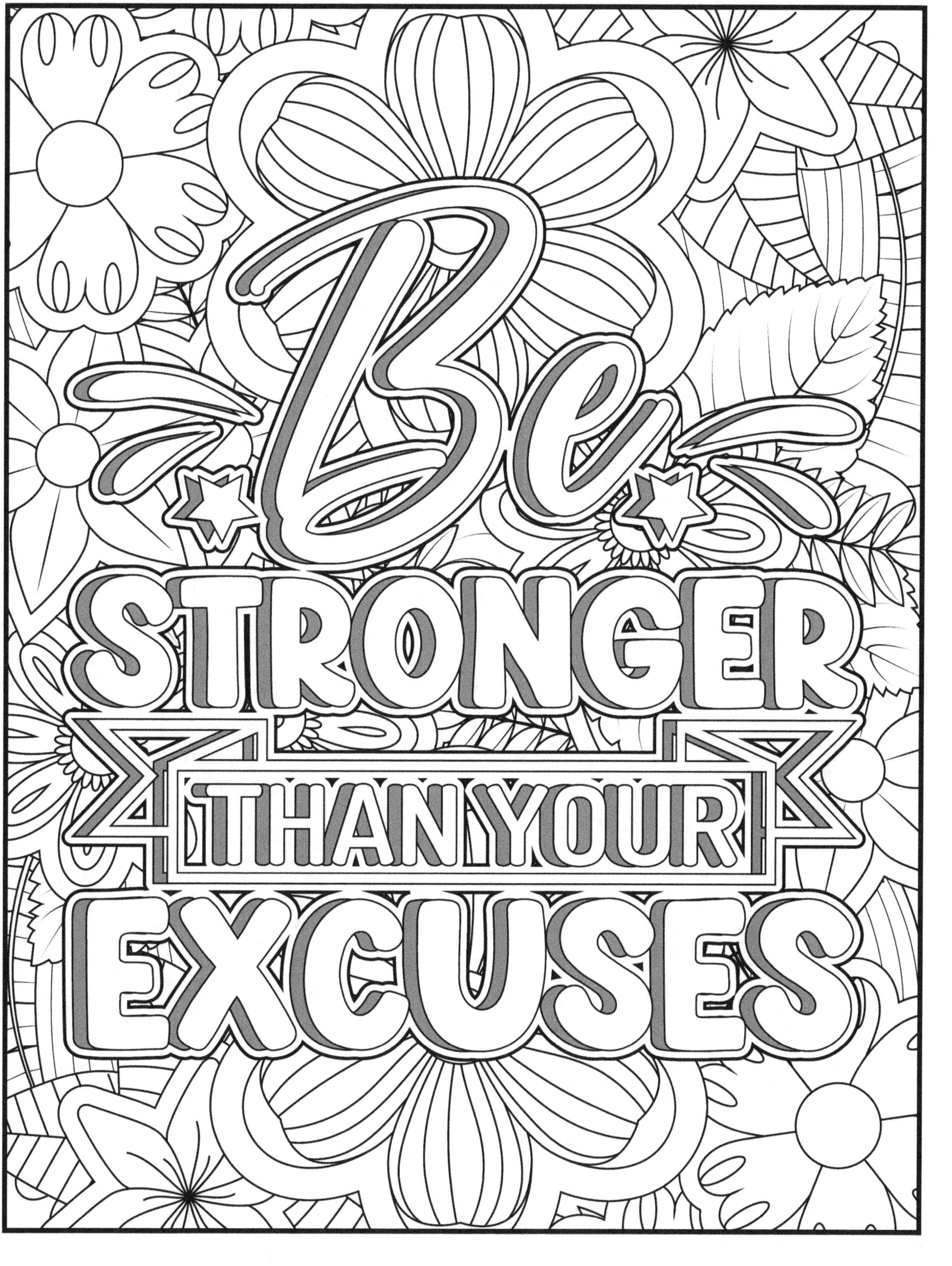
Be
STRONGER
THAN YOUR
EXCUSES

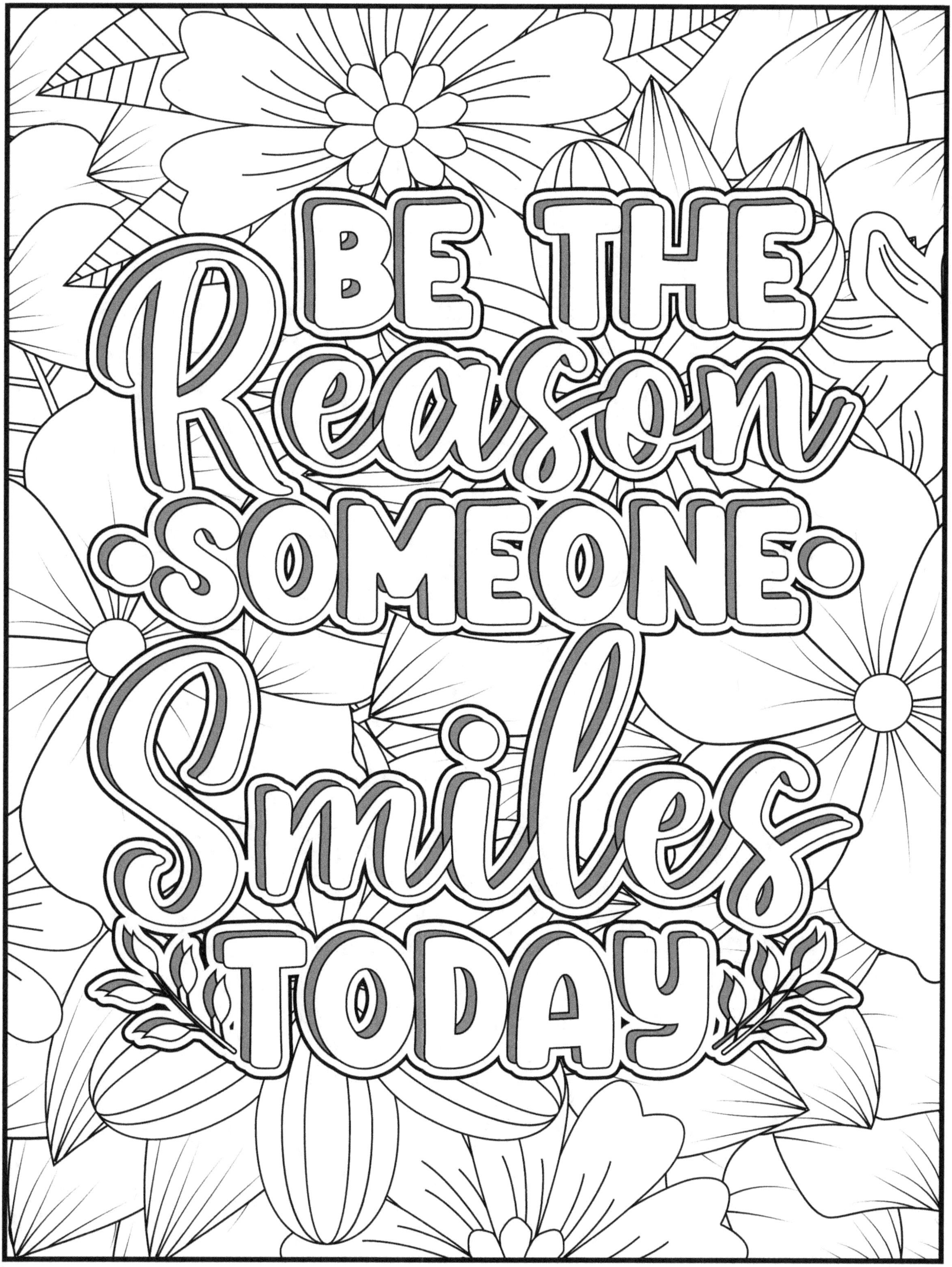
BE THE
Reason
SOMEONE
Smiles
TODAY

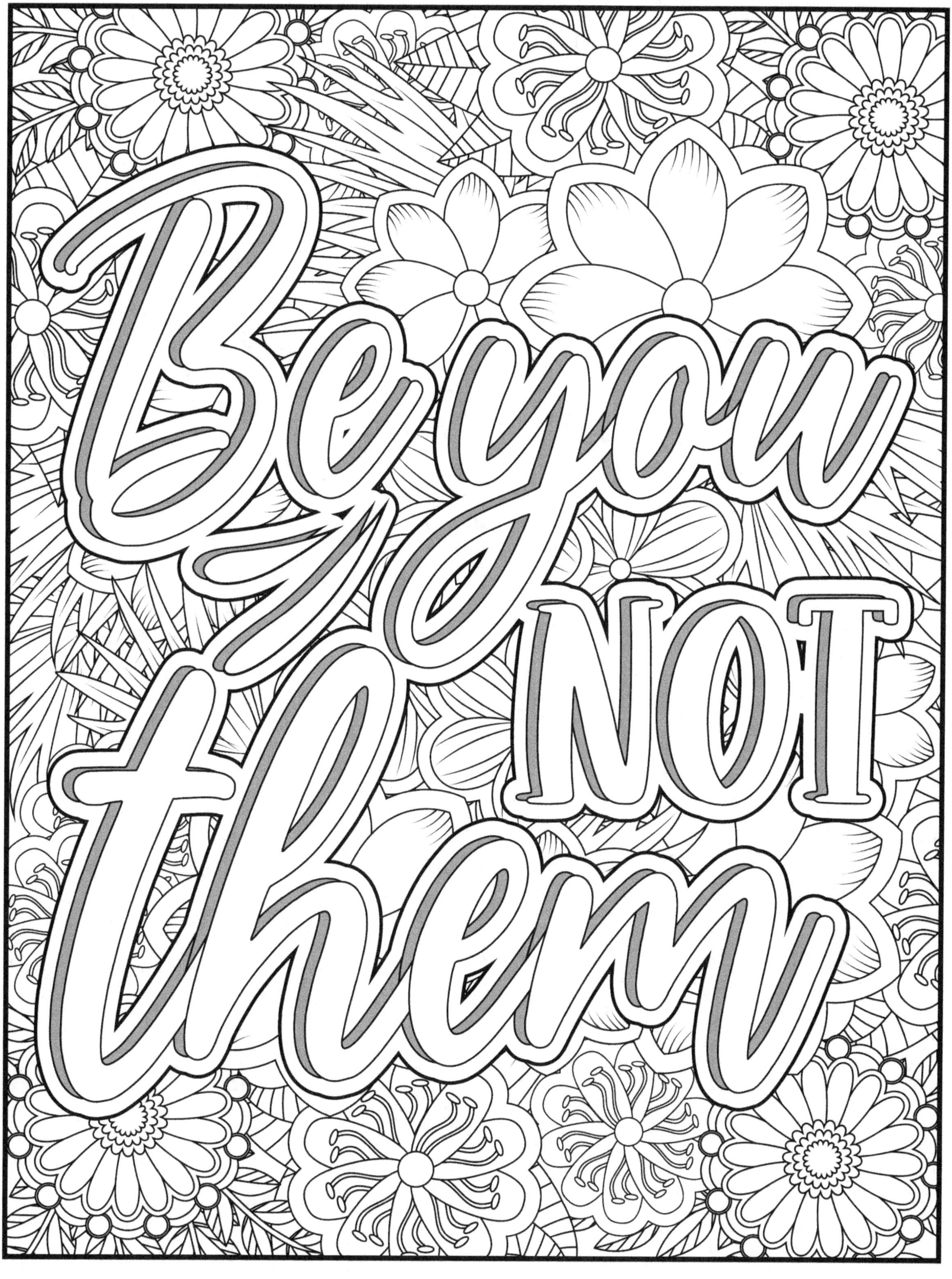
Be you
NOT
them

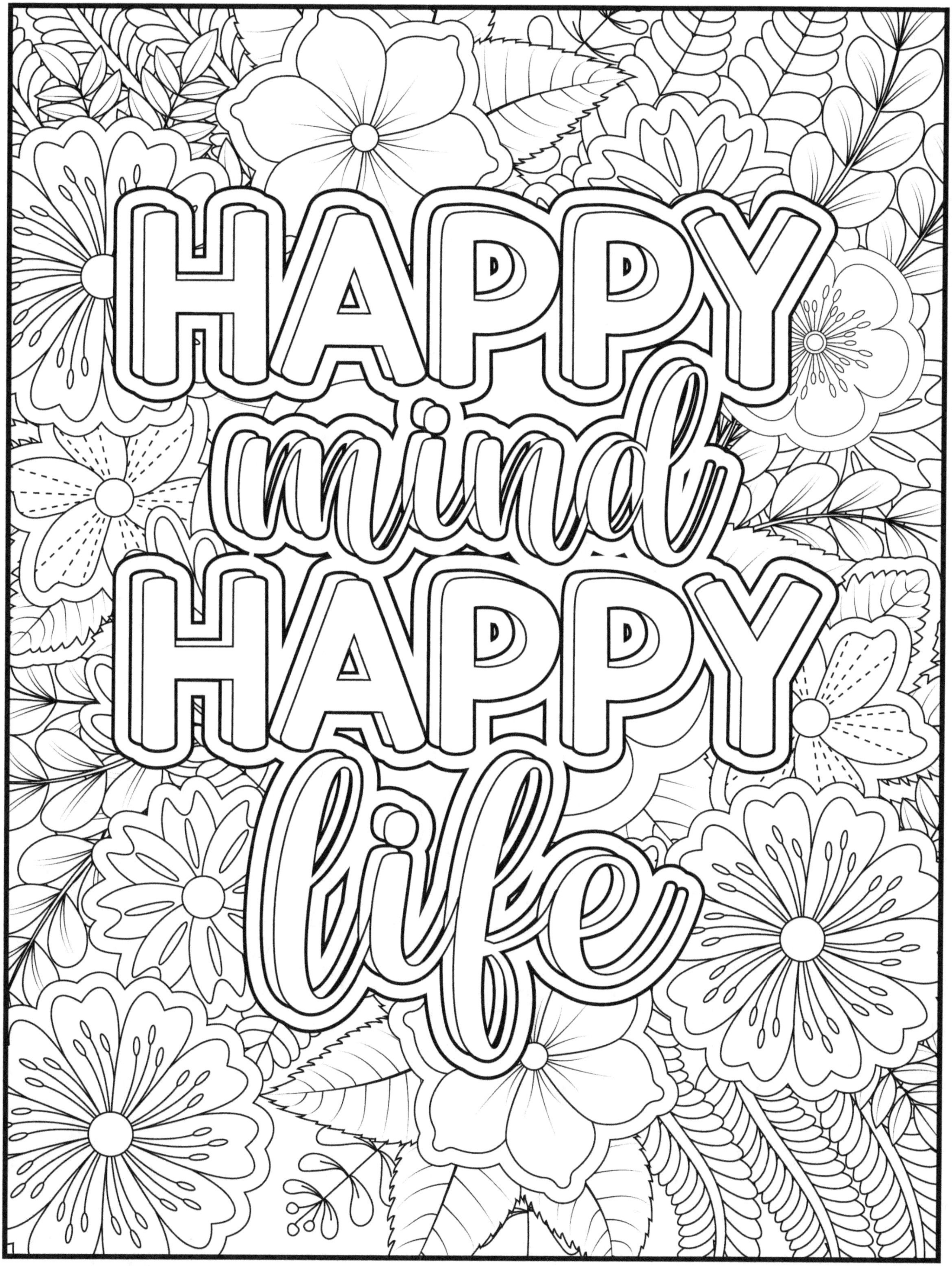
HAPPY
mind
HAPPY
life

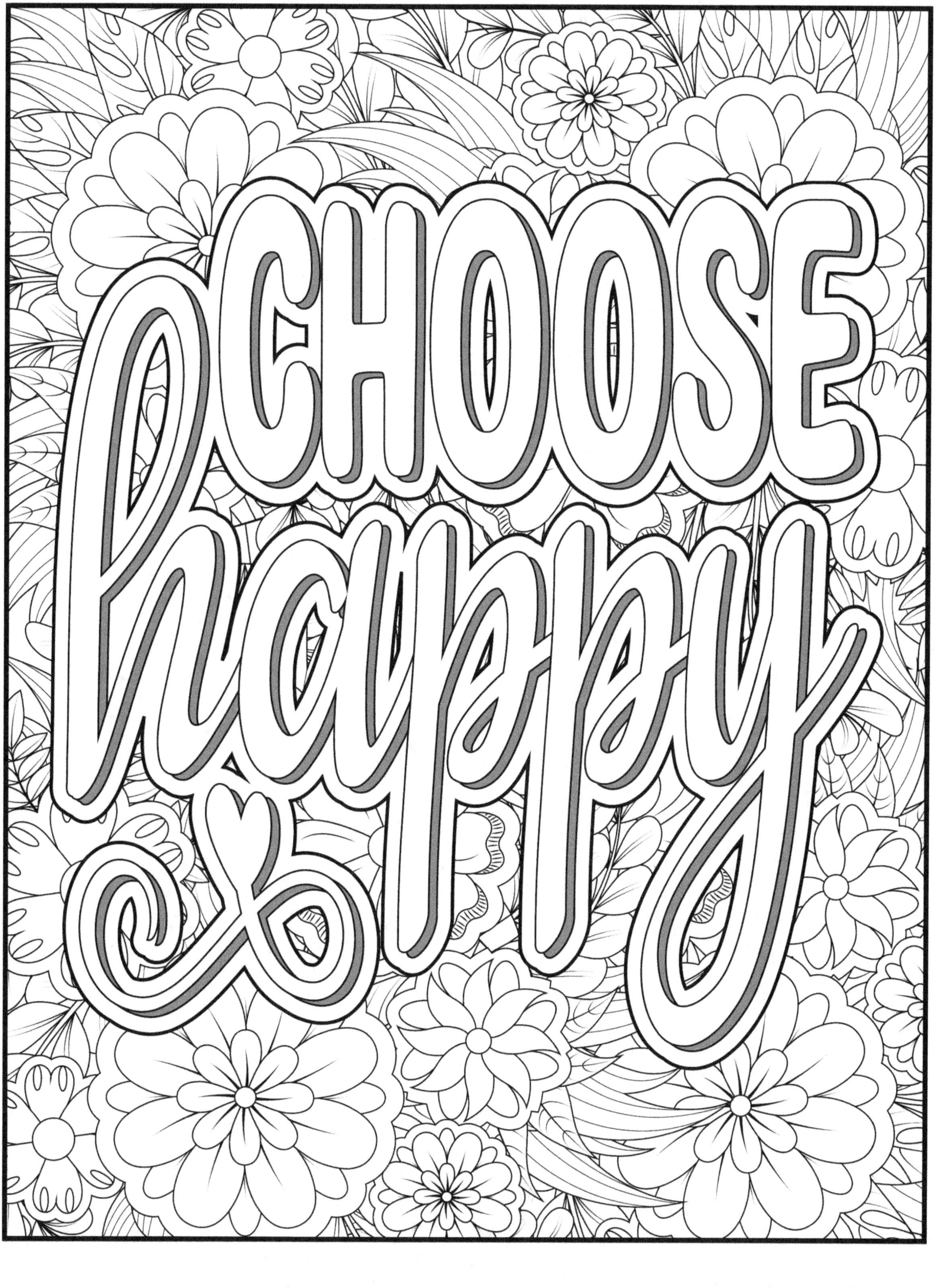
CHOOSE
happy

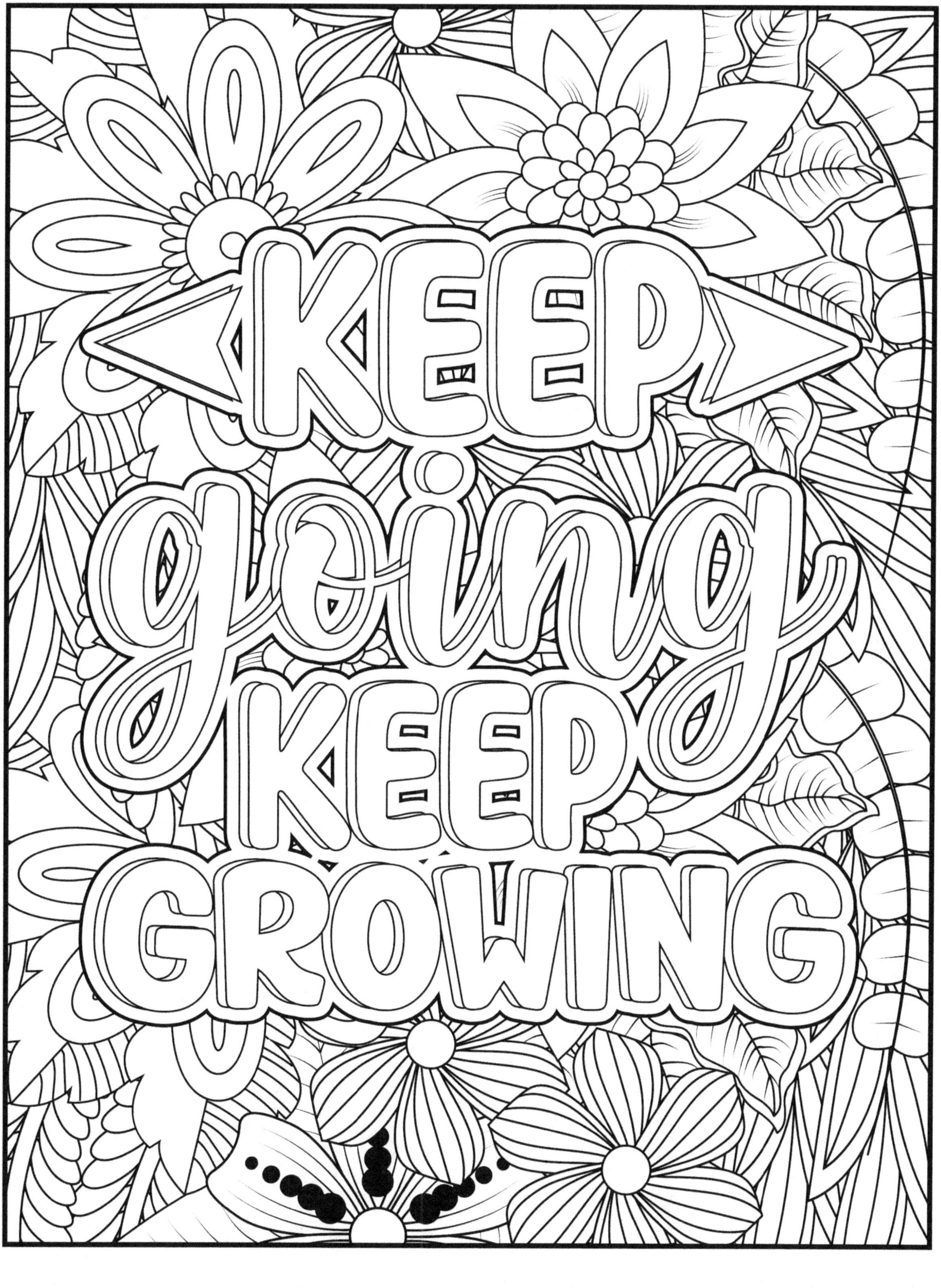
KEEP
going
KEEP
GROWING

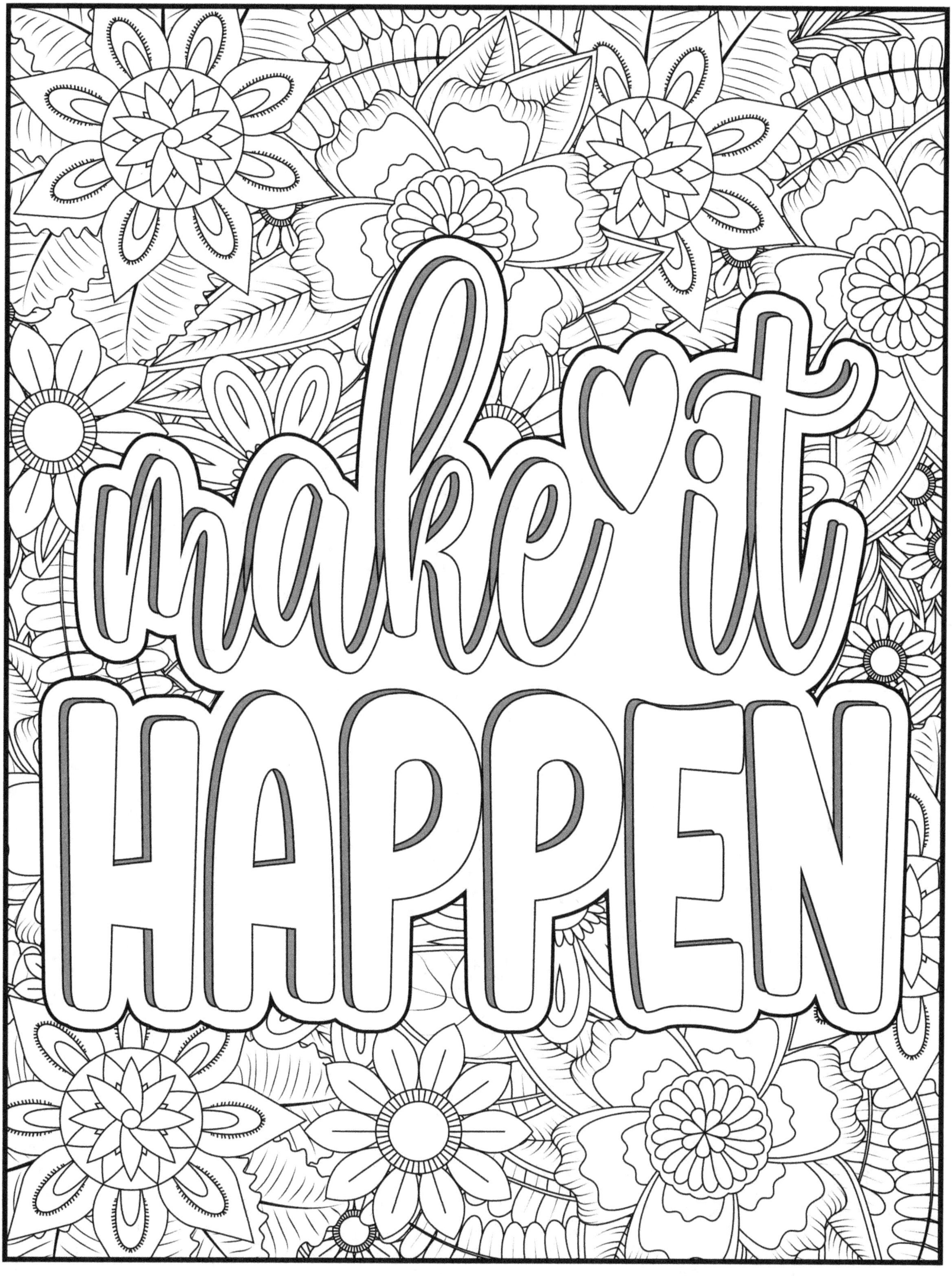
make it
HAPPEN

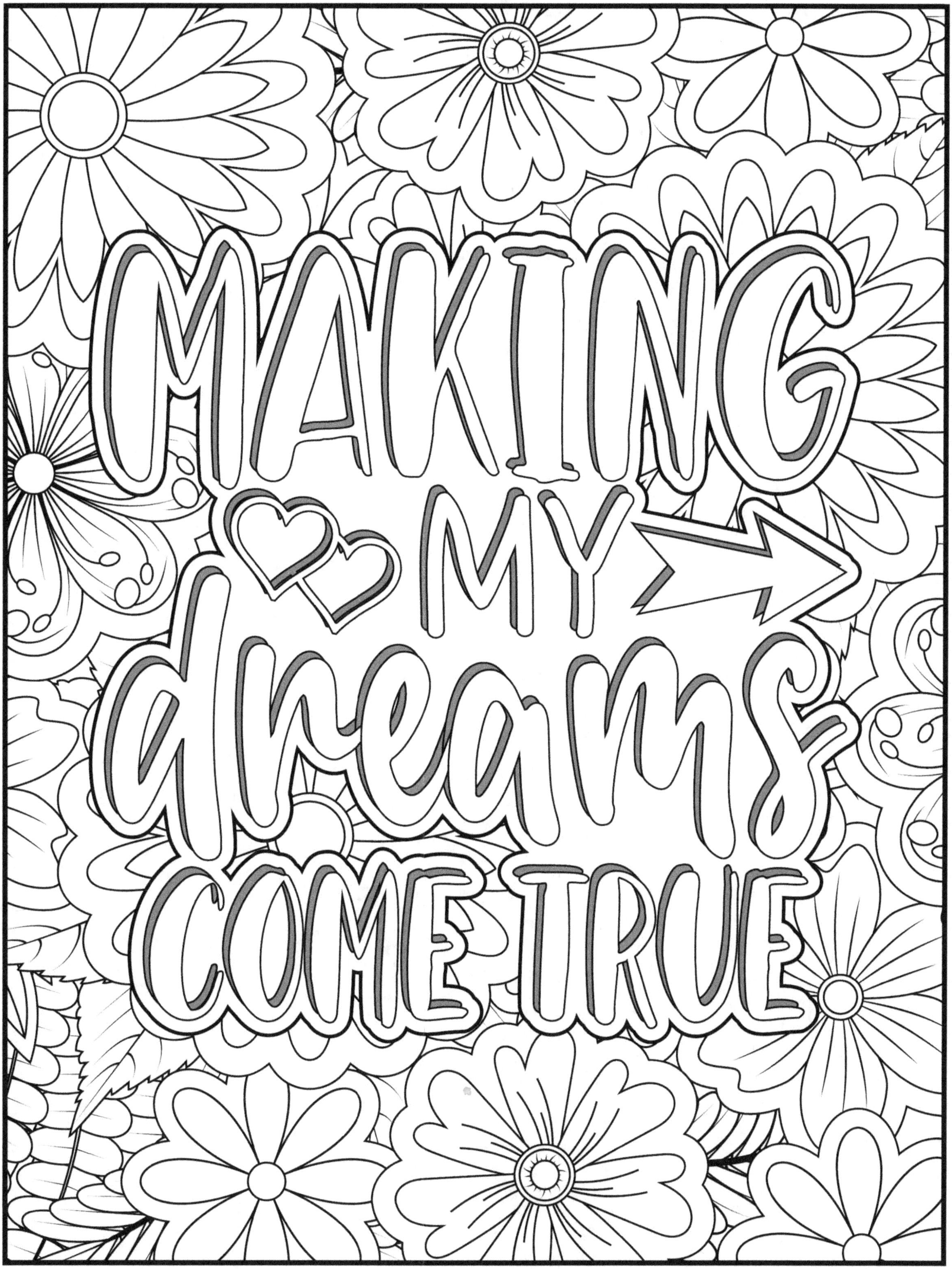
MAKING
MY
dreams
COME TRUE

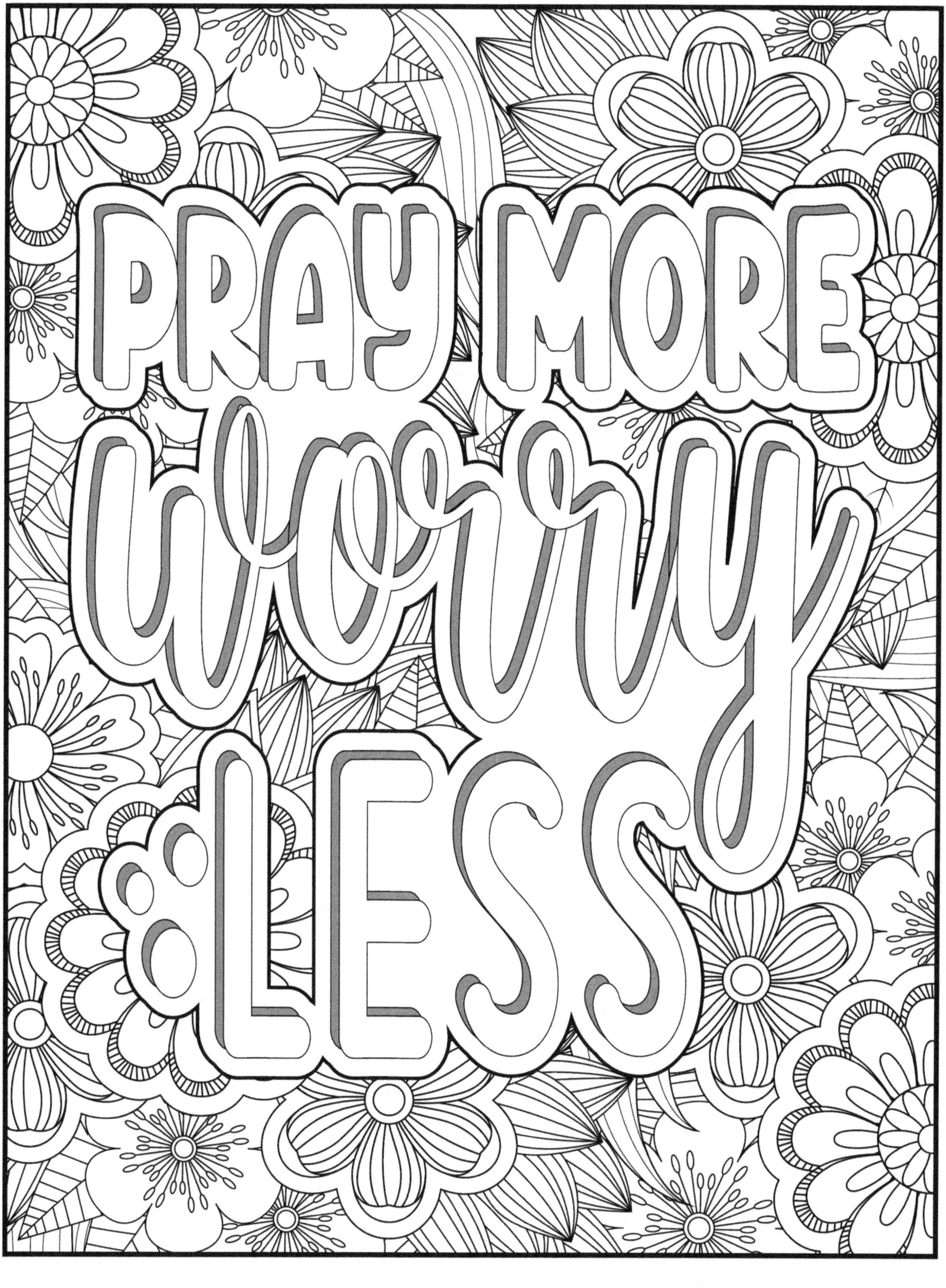
PRAY MORE
worry
LESS

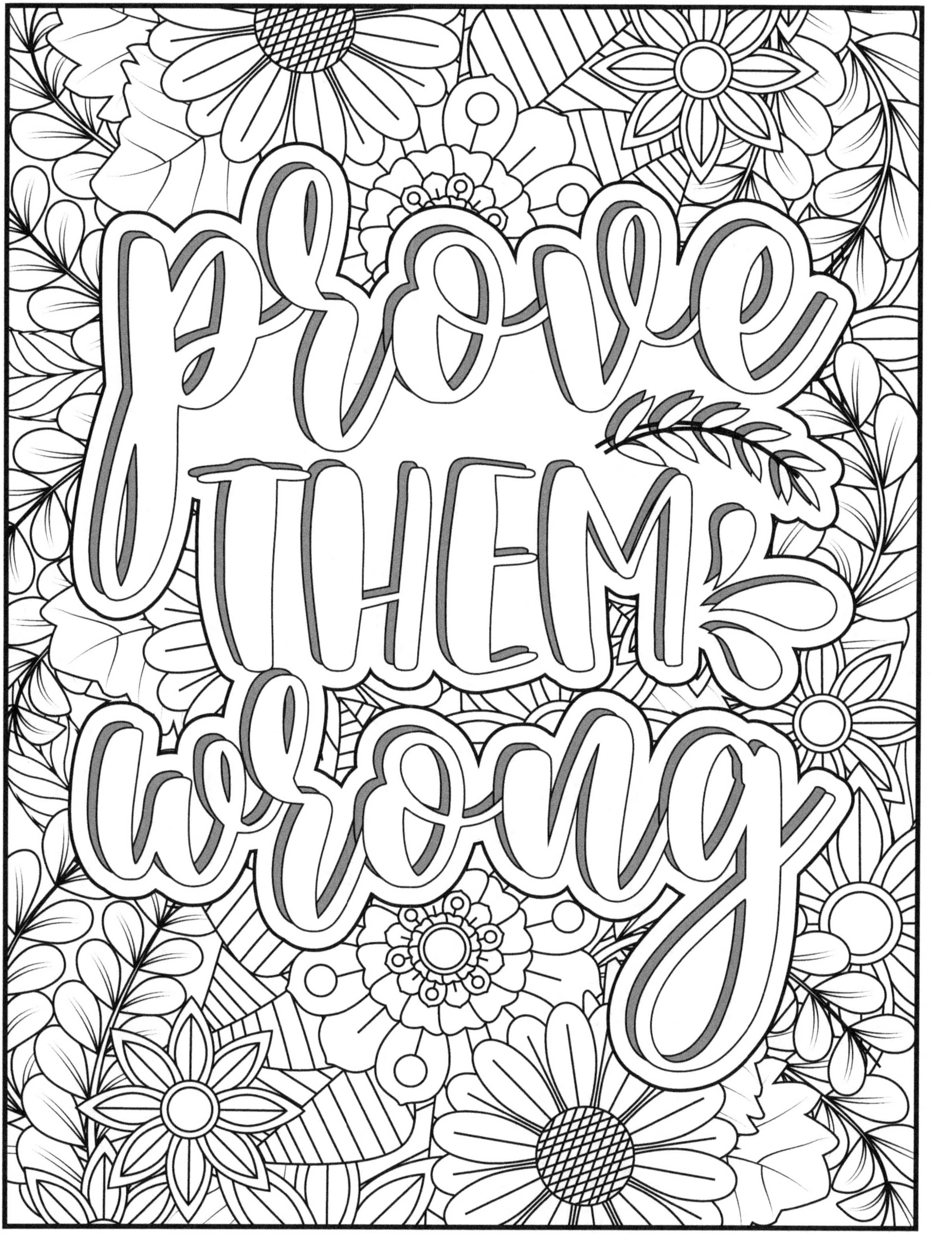
prove
THEM
wrong

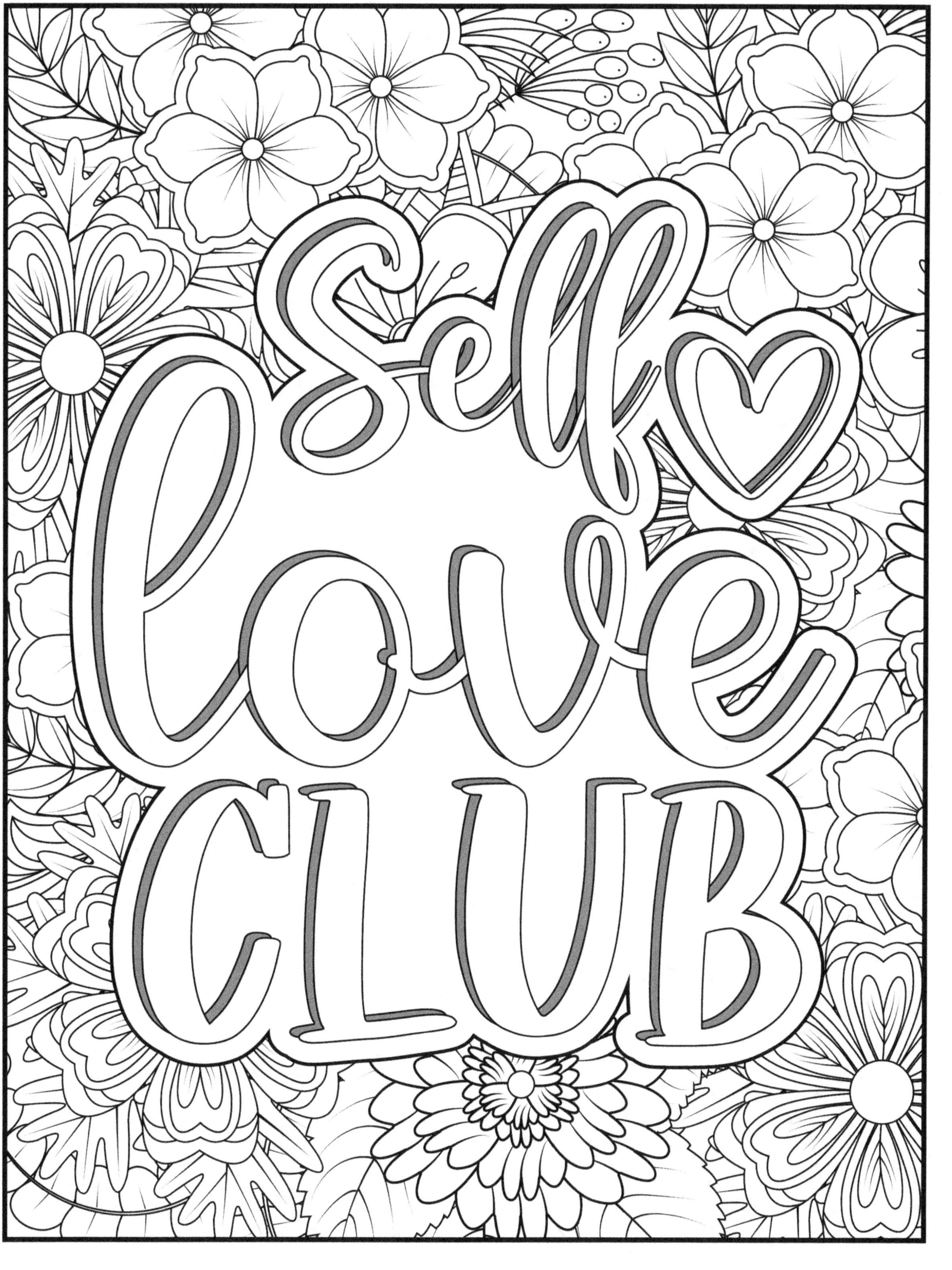
Self
love
CLUB

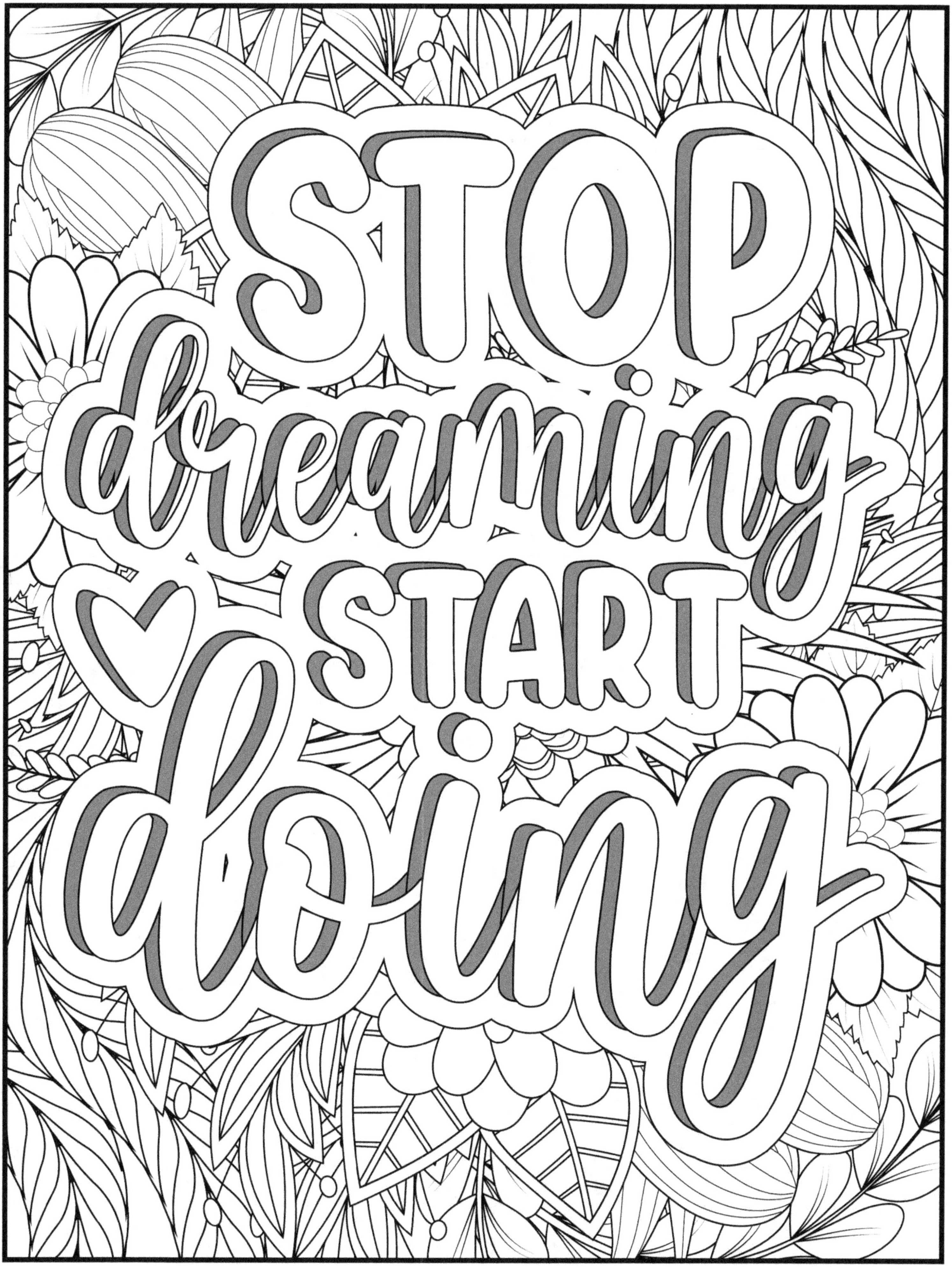
STOP
dreaming
START
doing

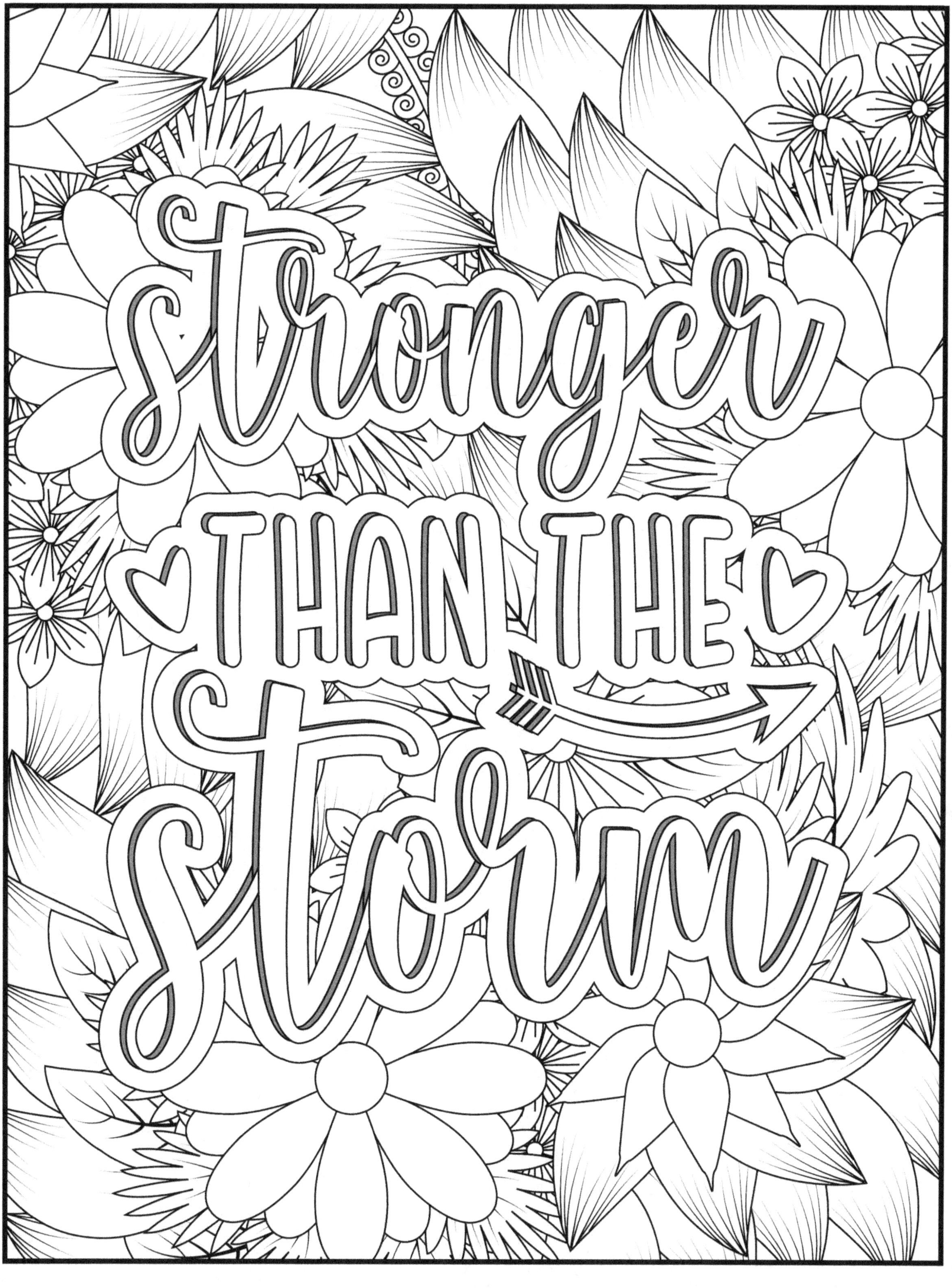
Stronger
THAN THE
Storm

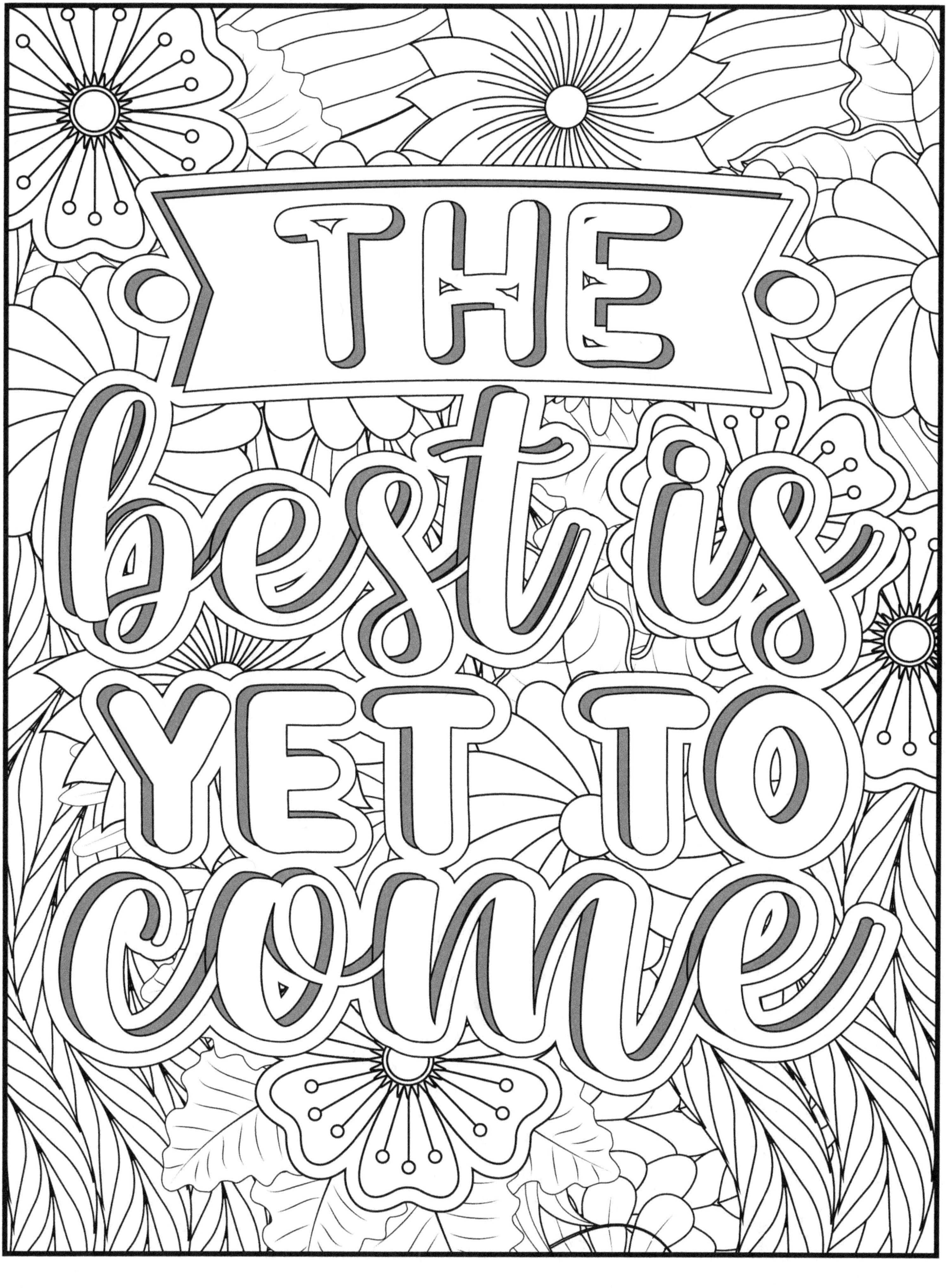
THE
best is
YET TO
come

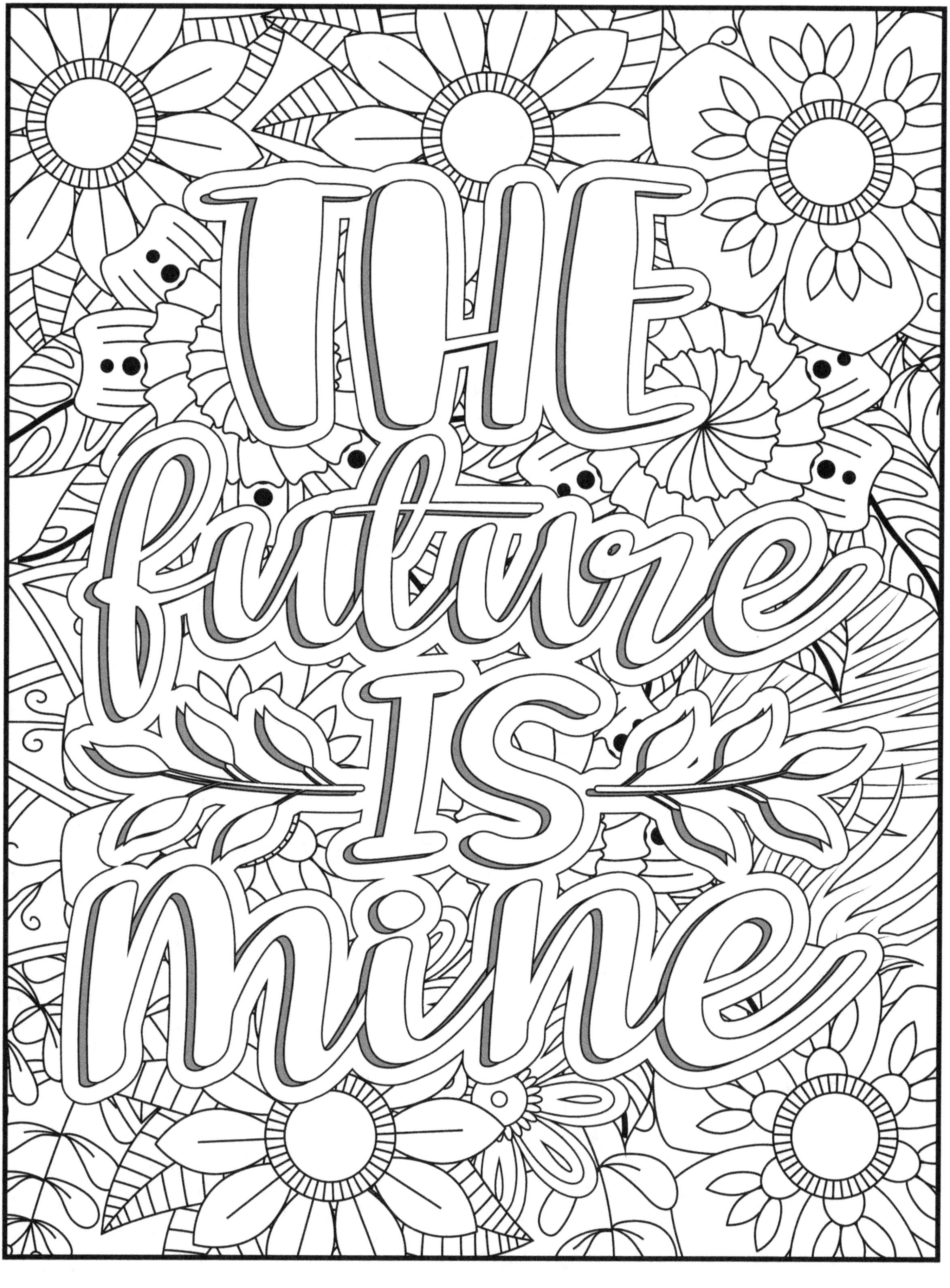
THE
future
IS
mine

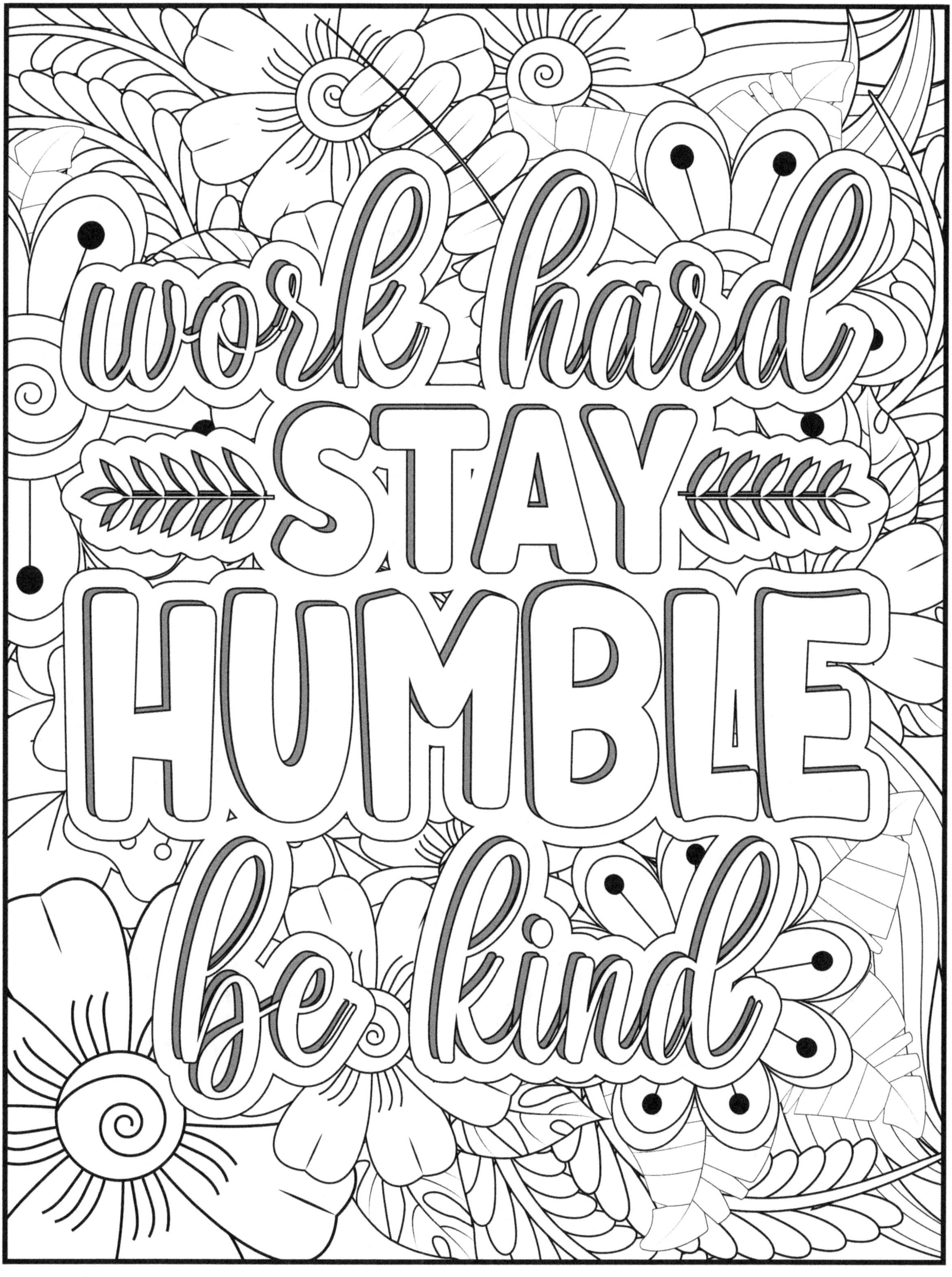
work hard
STAY
HUMBLE
be kind

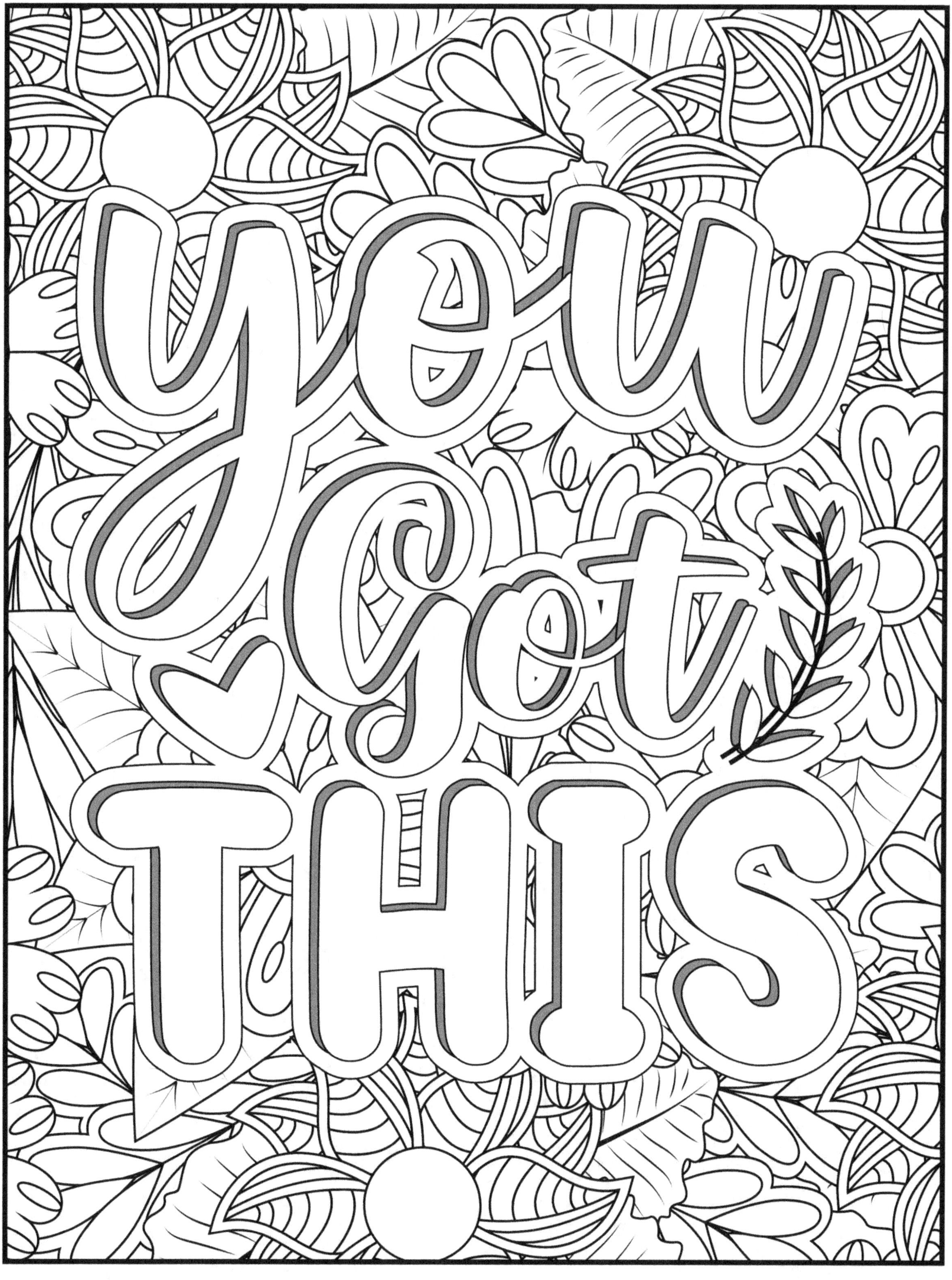
you
got
THIS

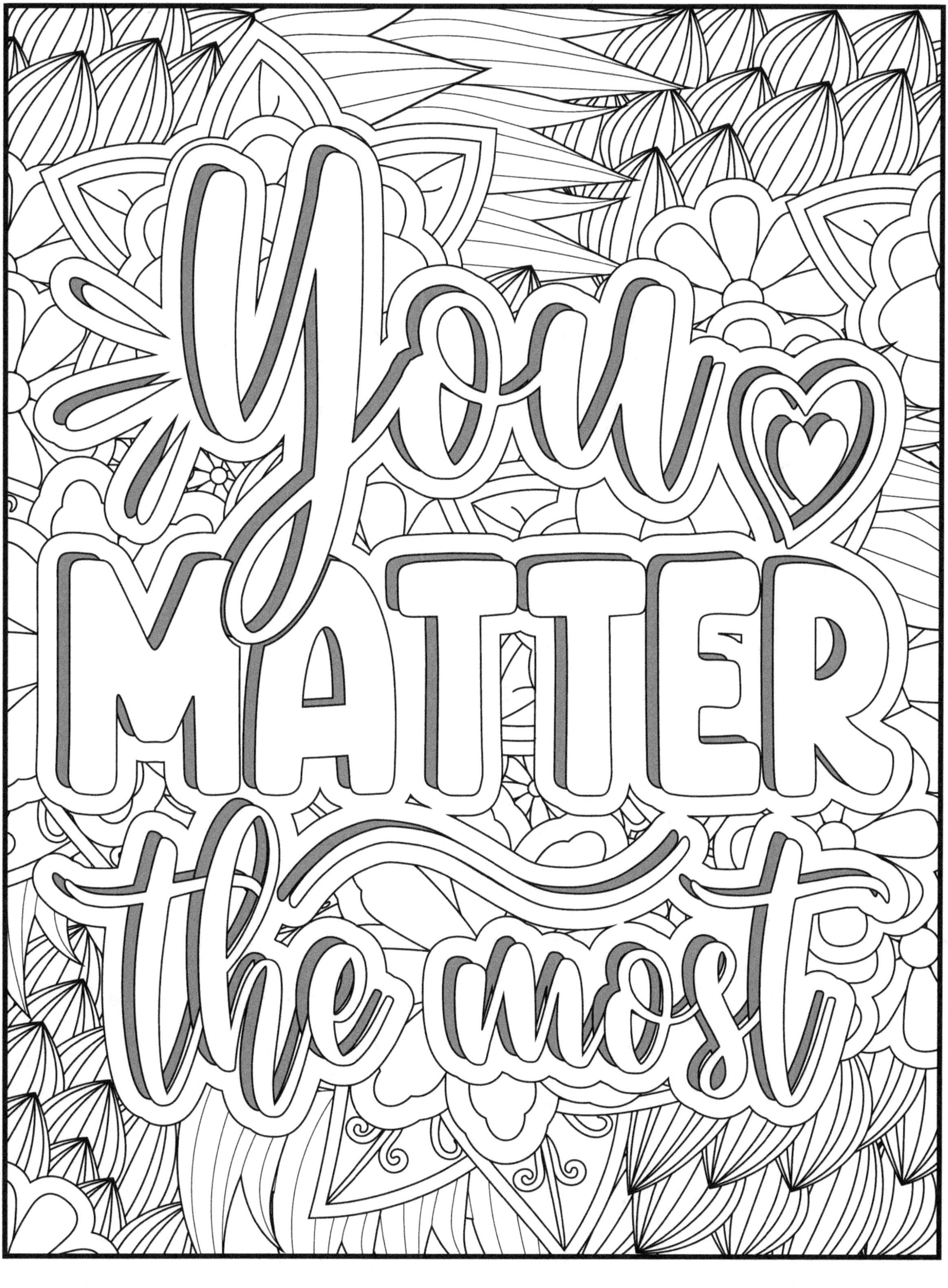
You
MATTER
the most

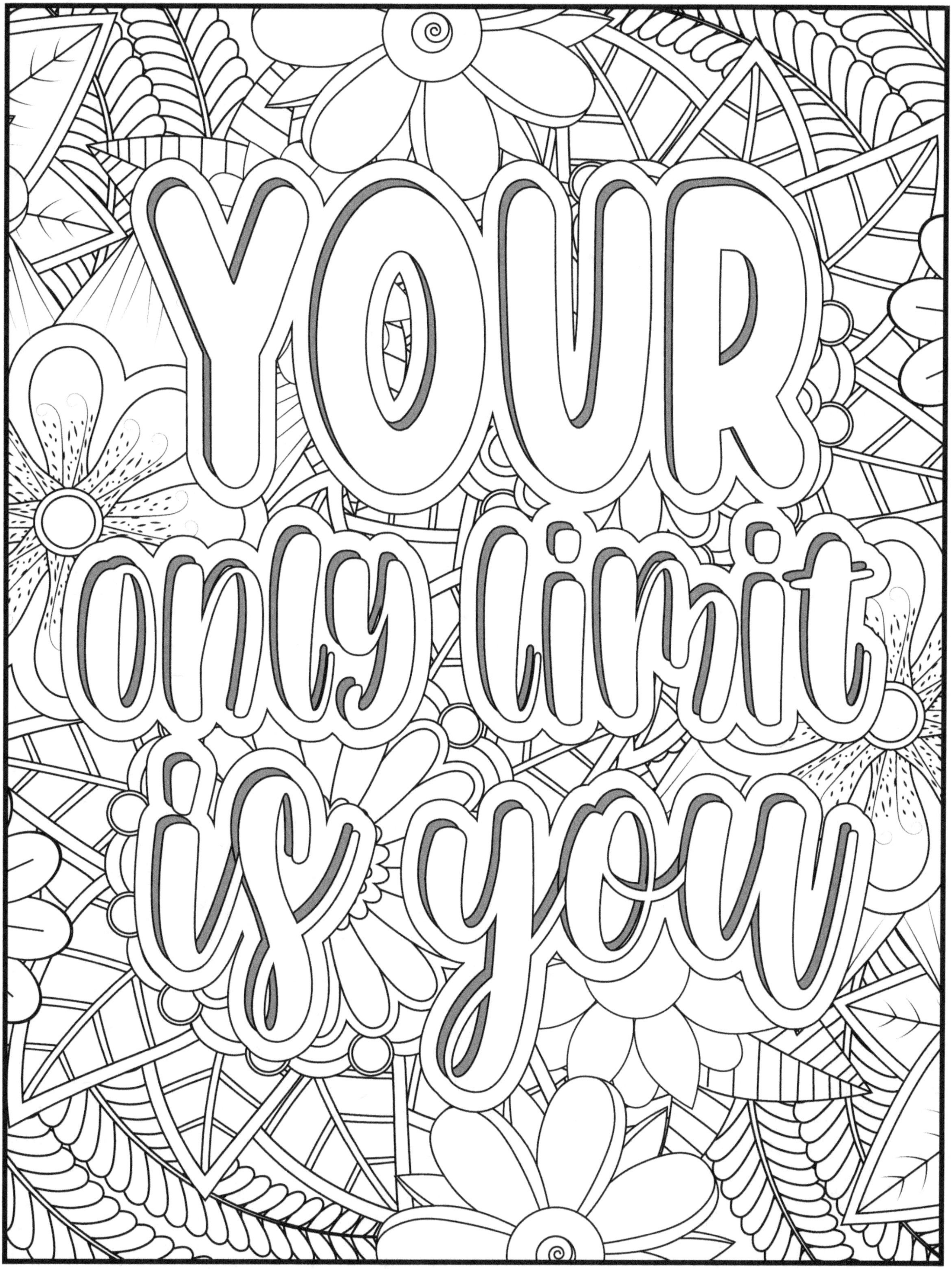
YOUR
only limit
is you

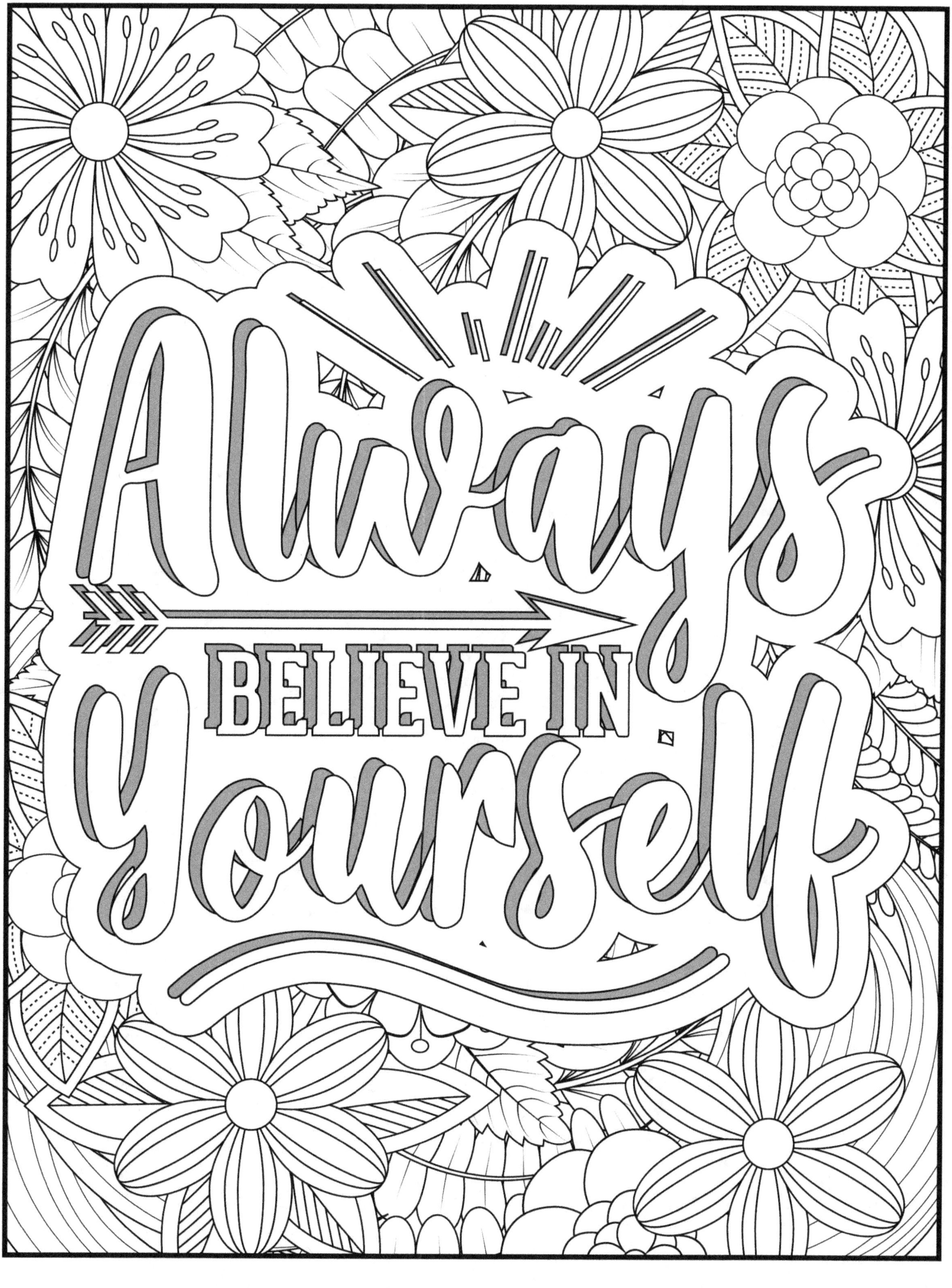
Always
BELIEVE IN
Yourself

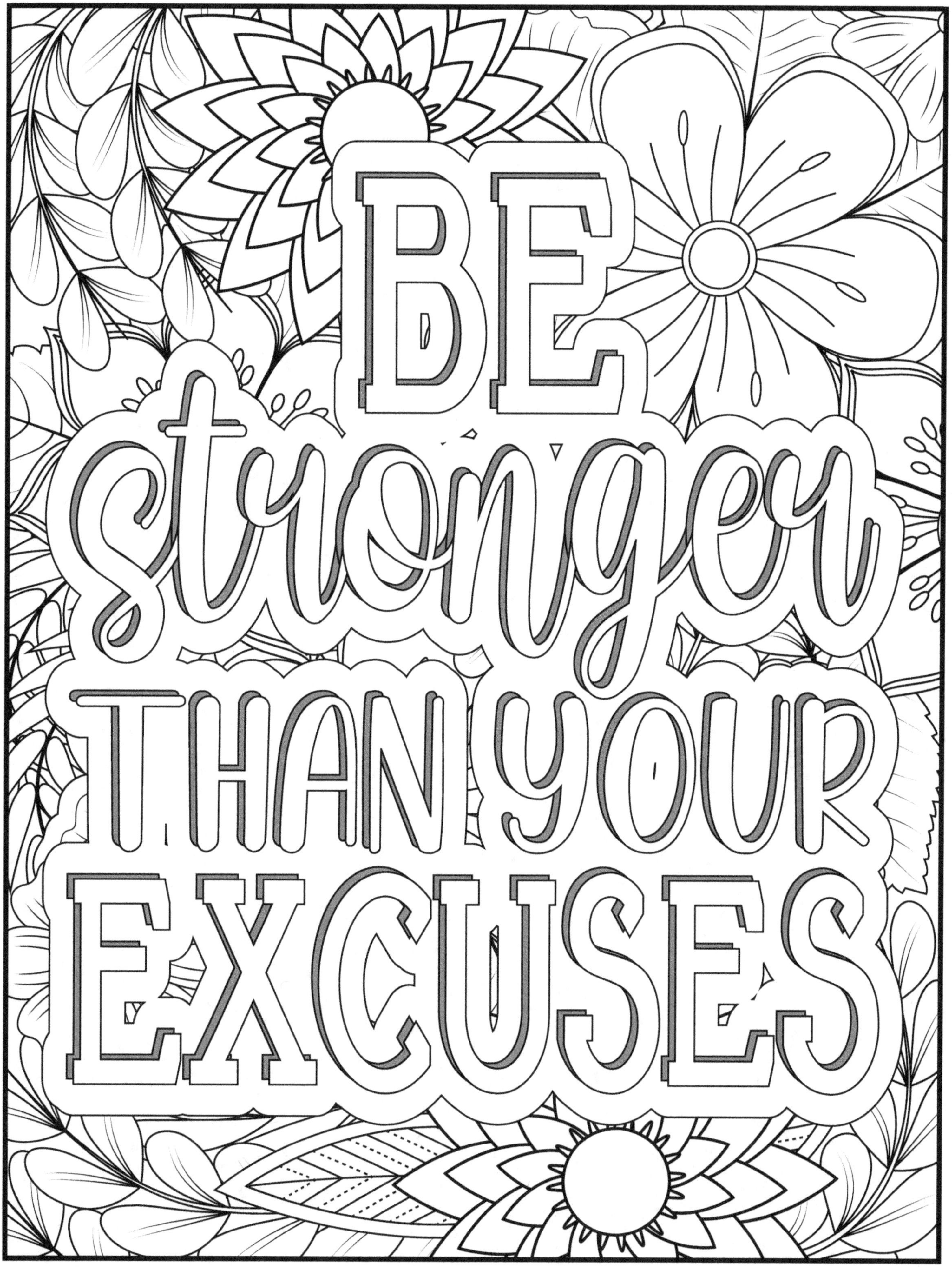
BE
stronger
THAN YOUR
EXCUSES

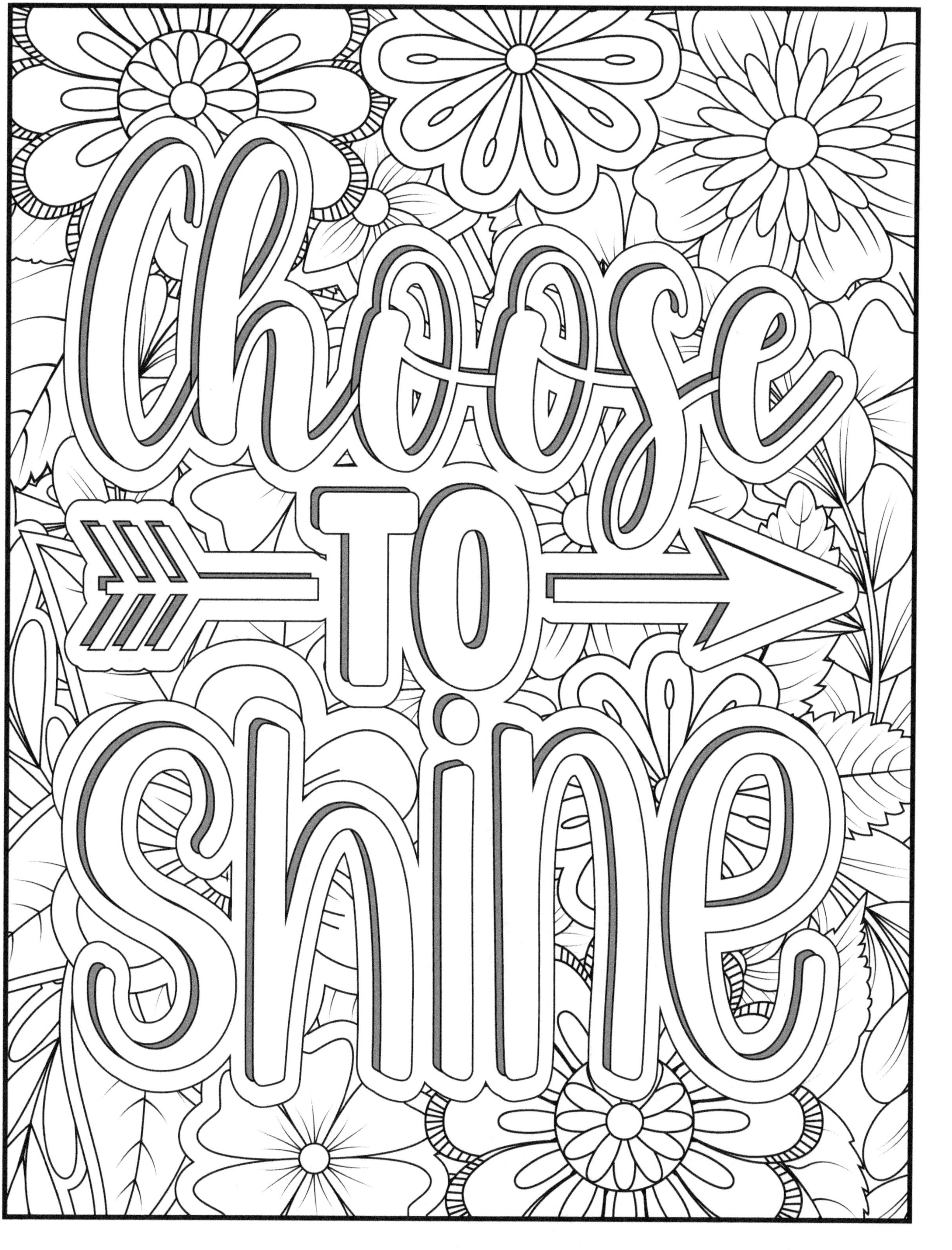
Choose
TO
Shine

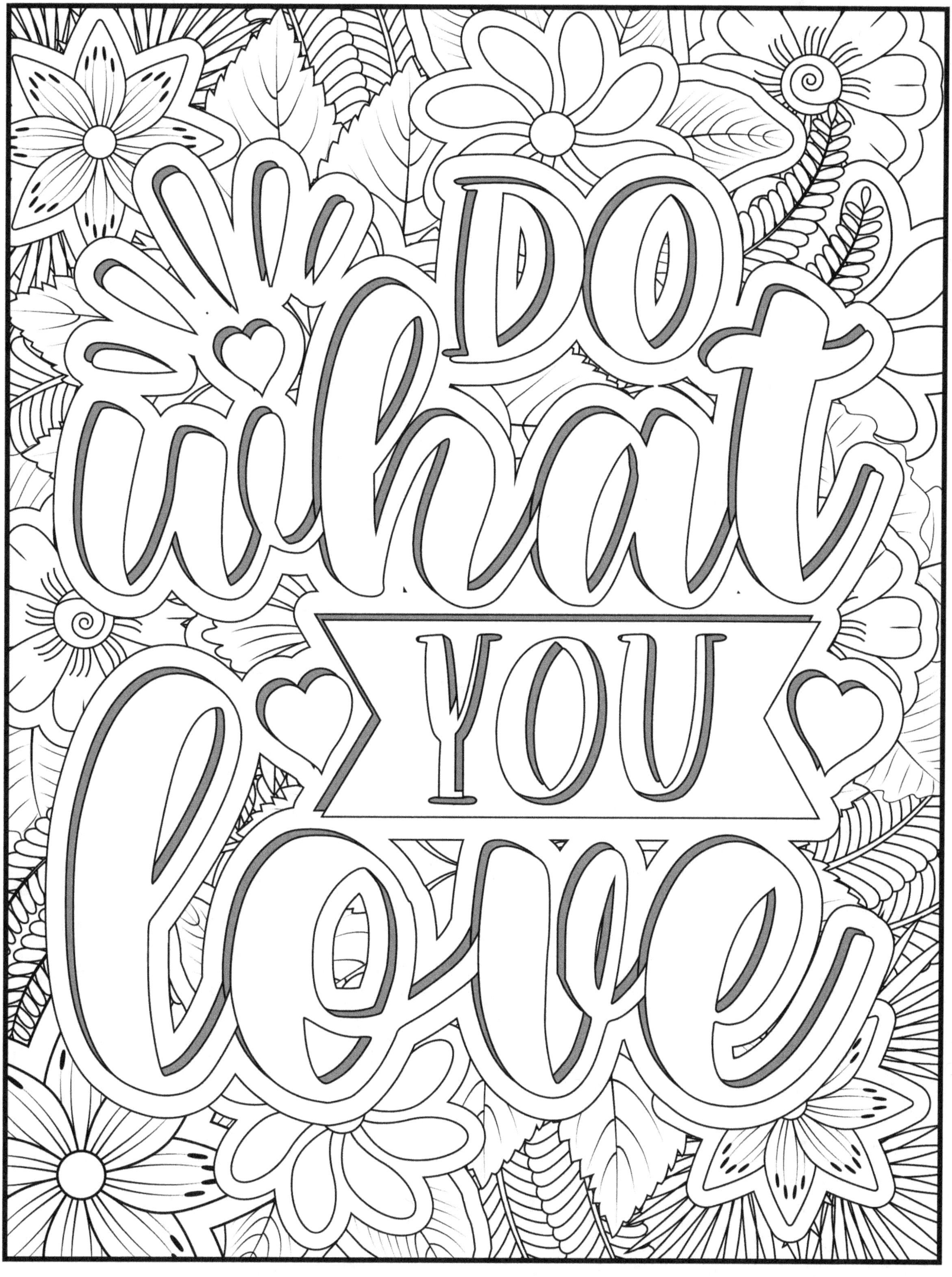
DO
what
YOU
love

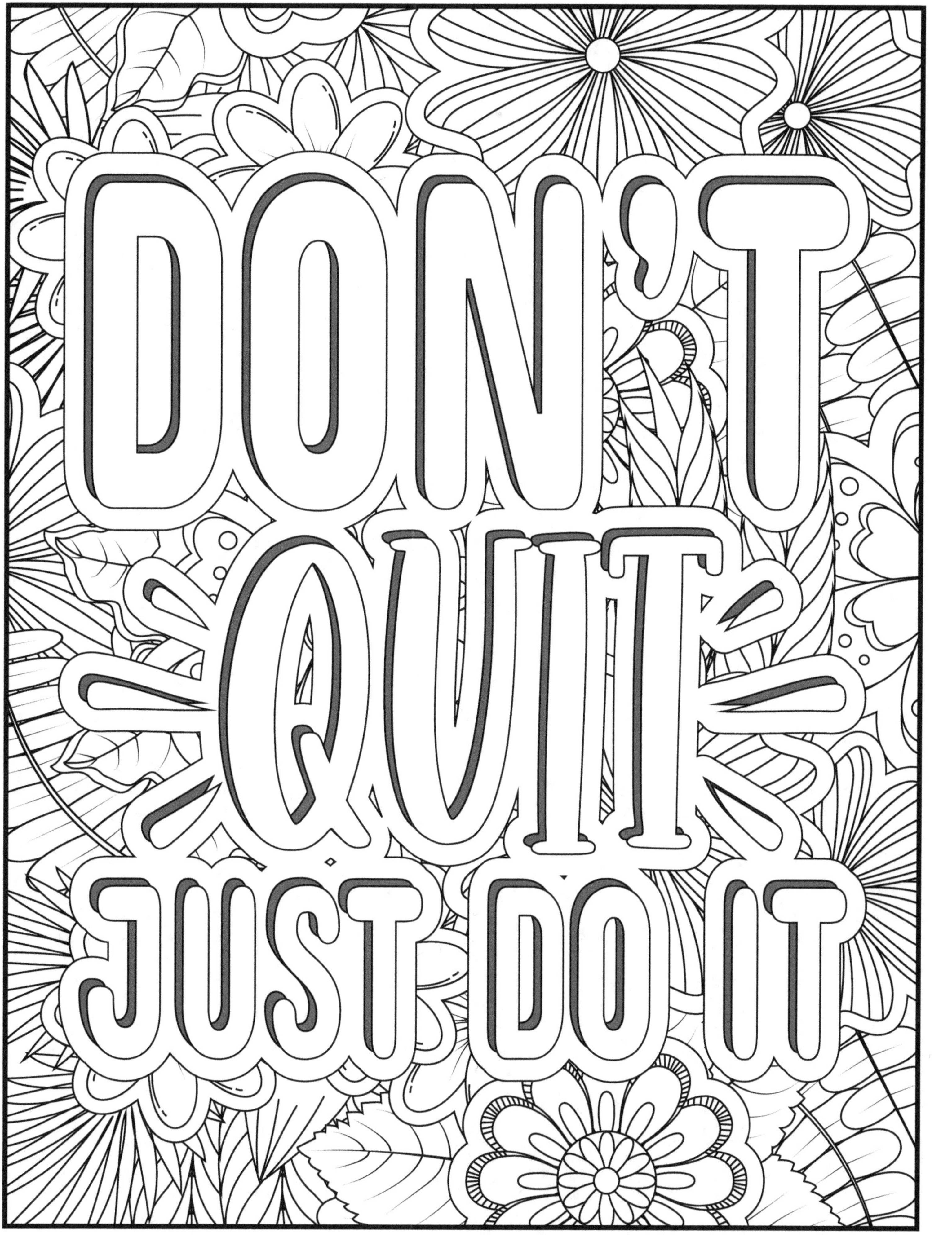
DON'T QUIT
JUST DO IT

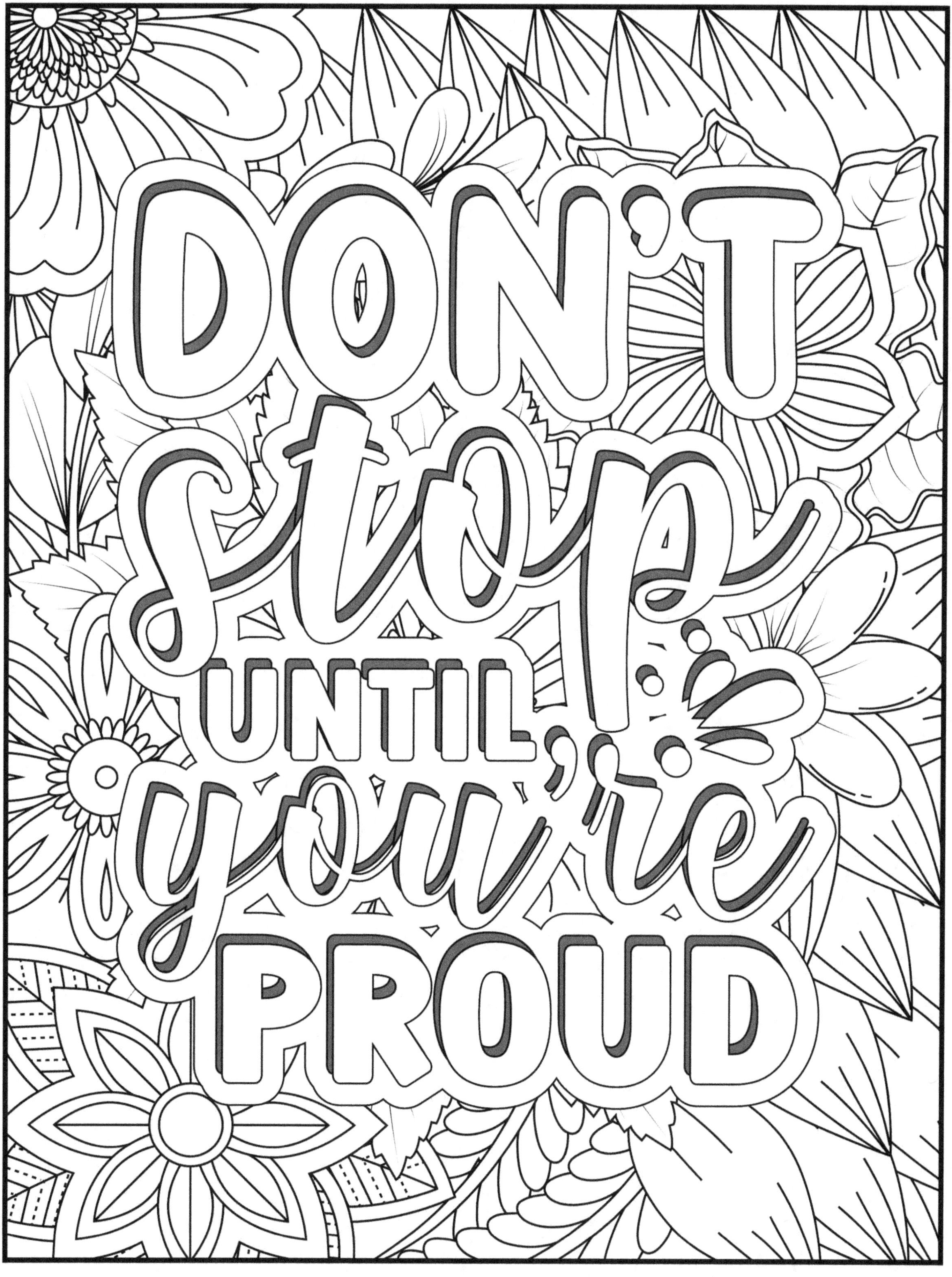
DON'T
stop
UNTIL
you're
PROUD

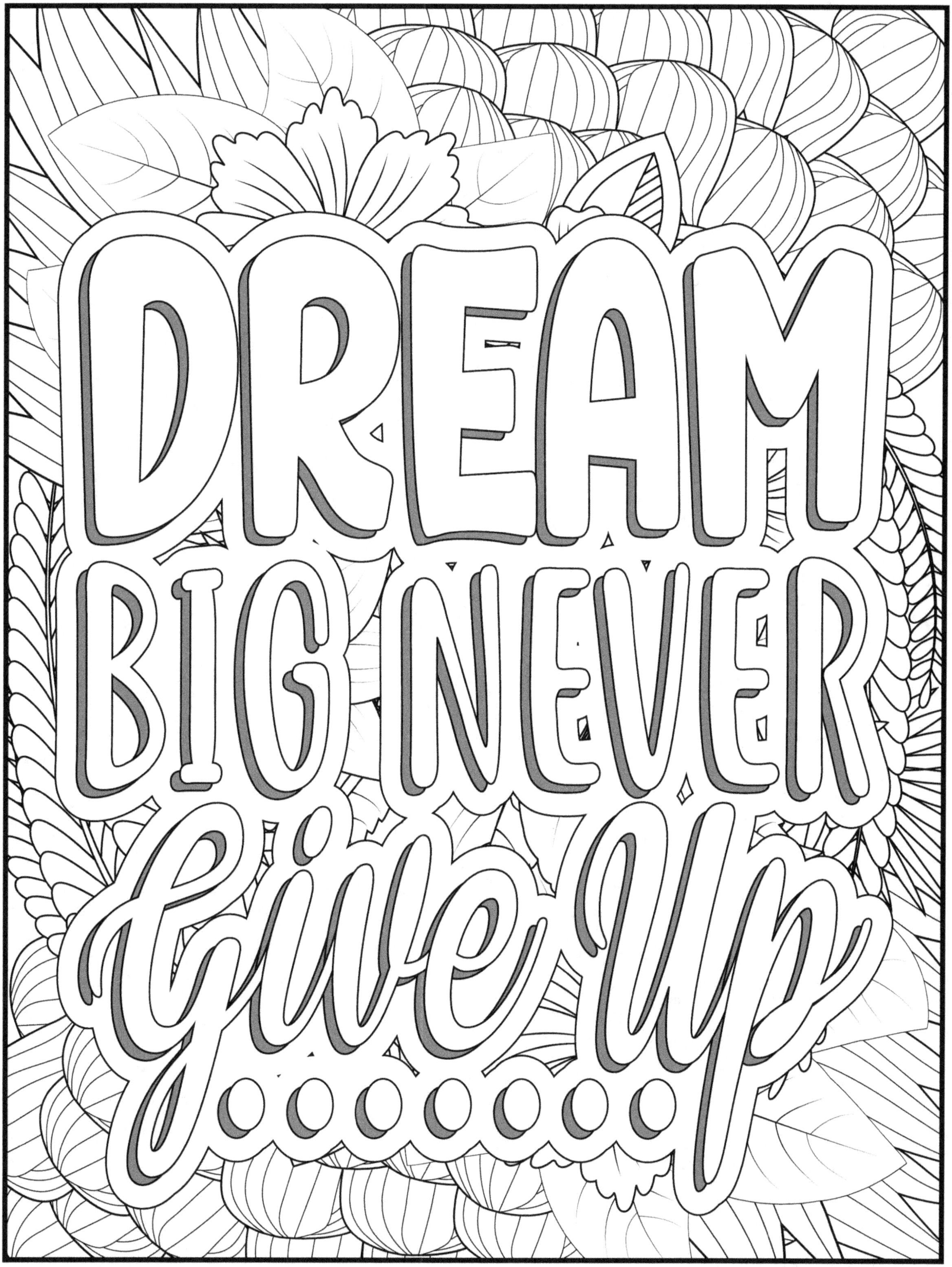
DREAM
BIG NEVER
Give Up

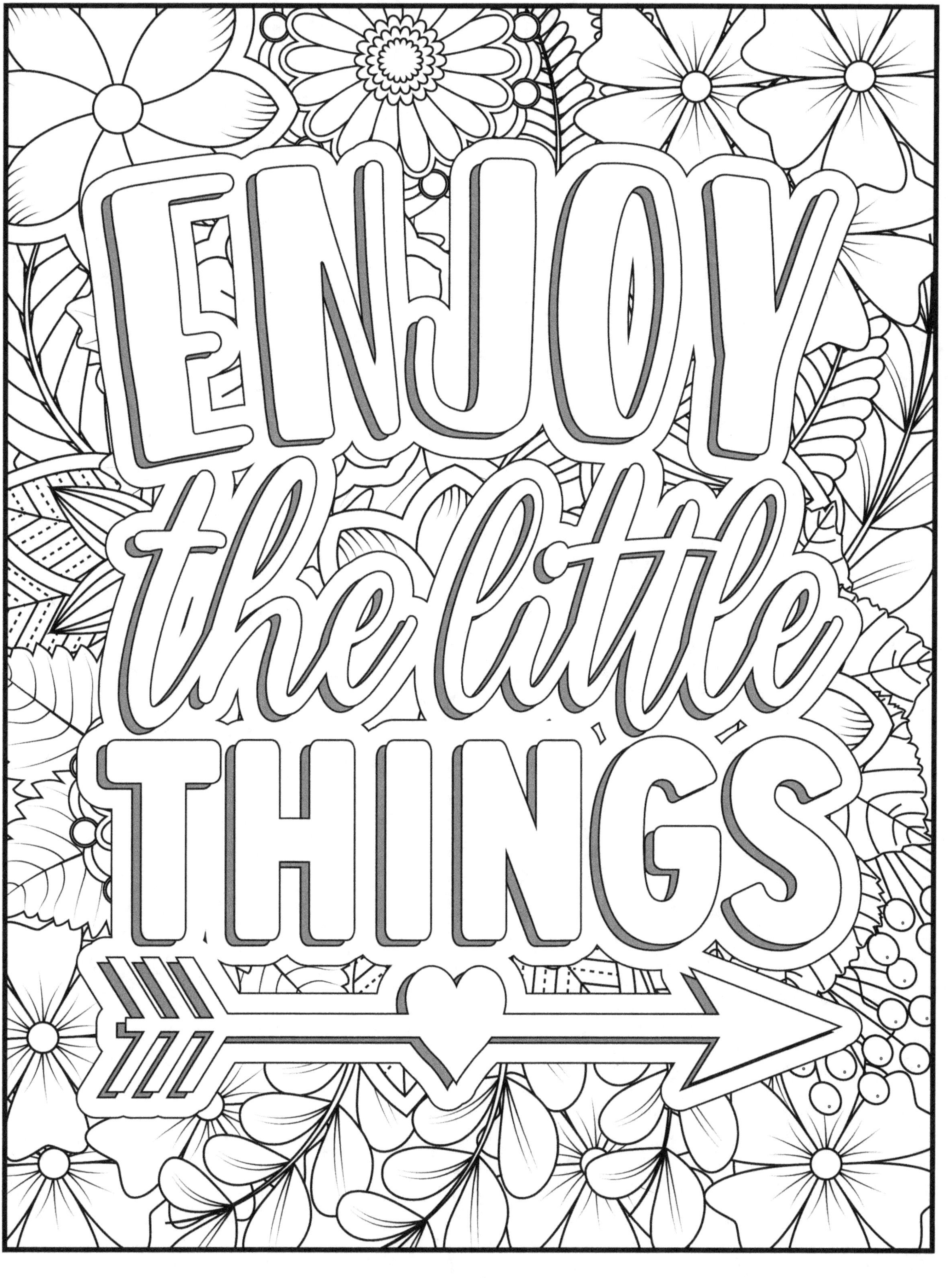
ENJOY
the little
THINGS

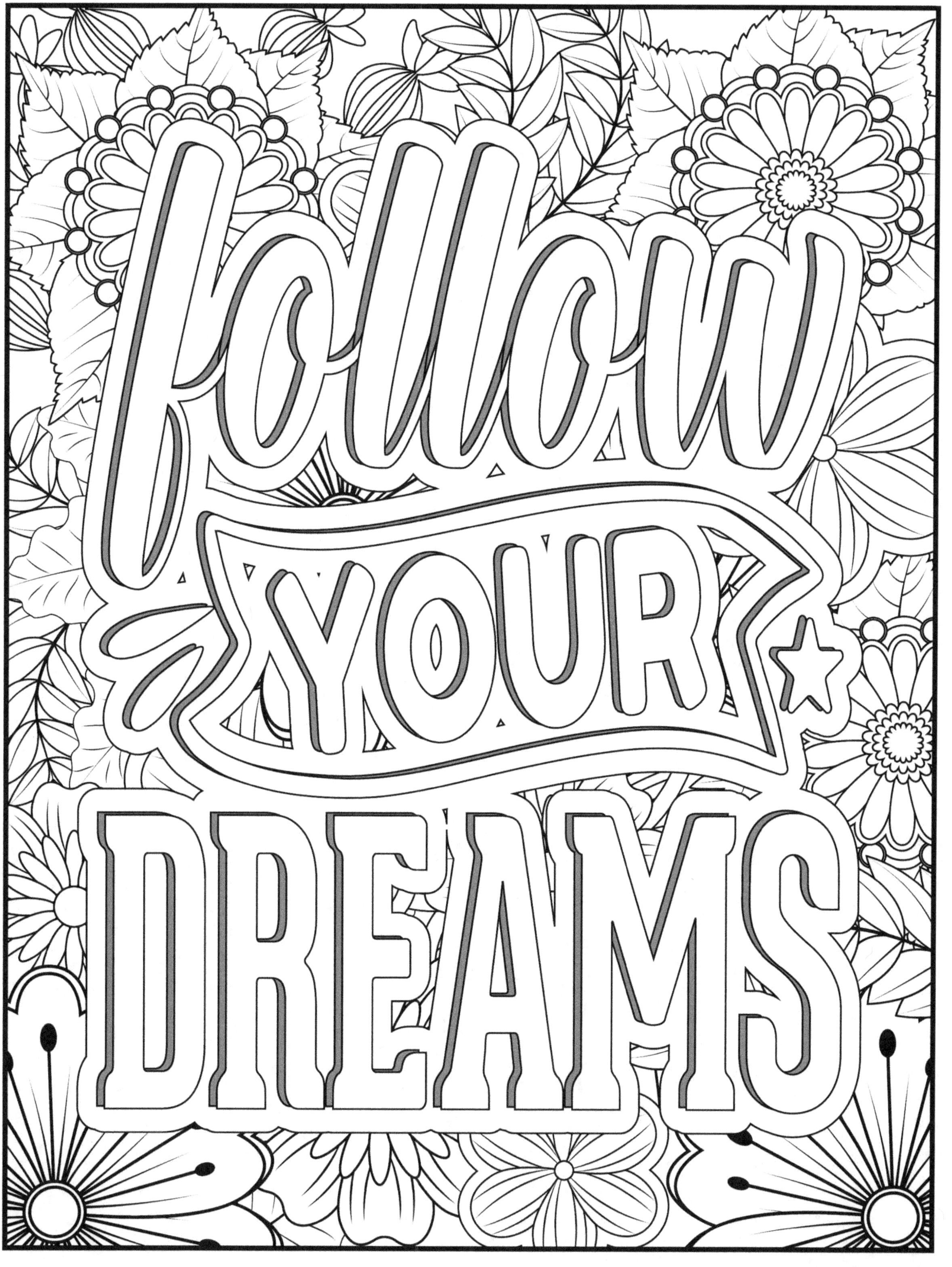
follow
YOUR
DREAMS

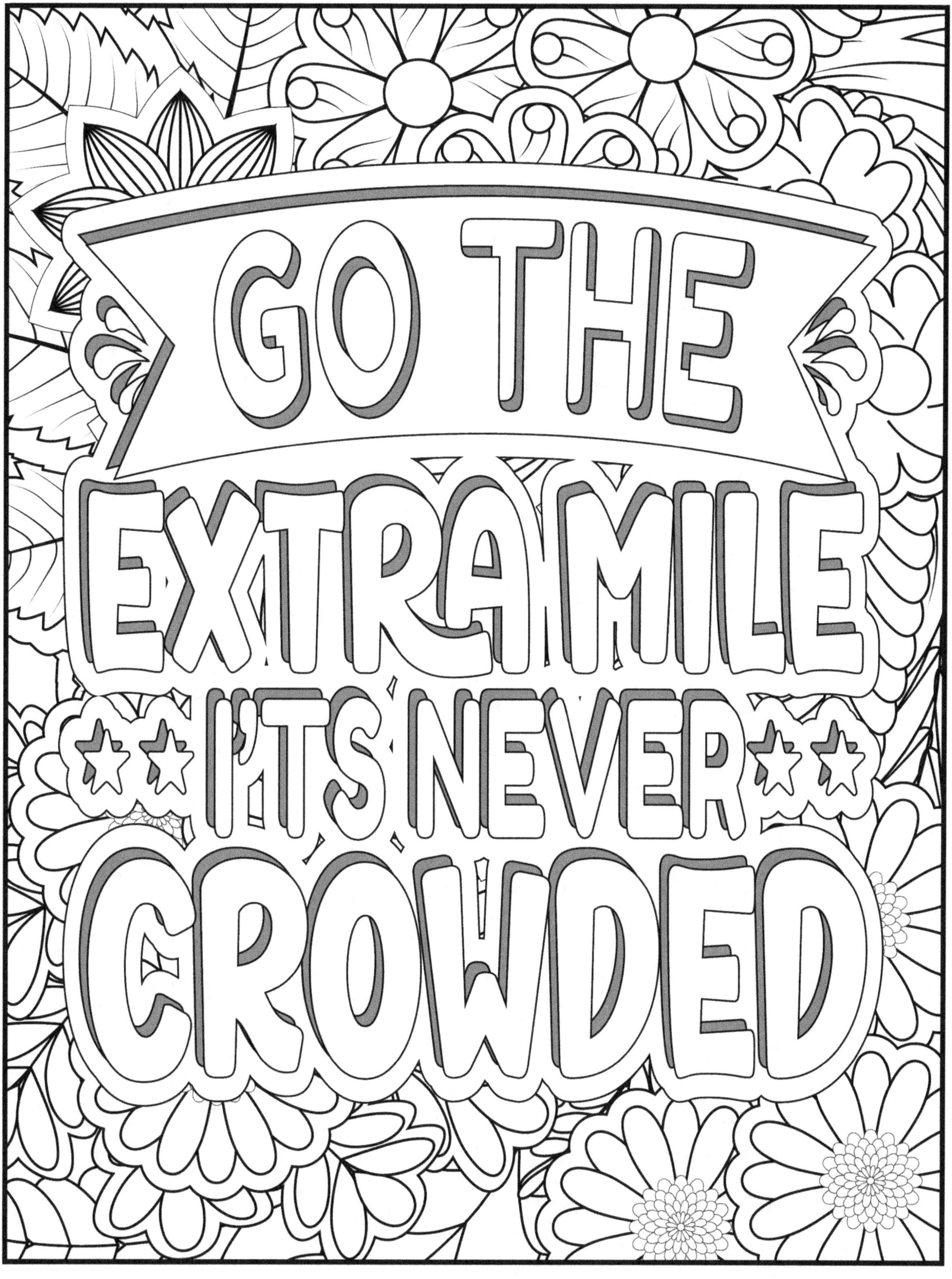
GO THE
EXTRA MILE
IT'S NEVER
CROWDED

IT'S JUST
A
BAD DAY
NOT A
BAD LIFE

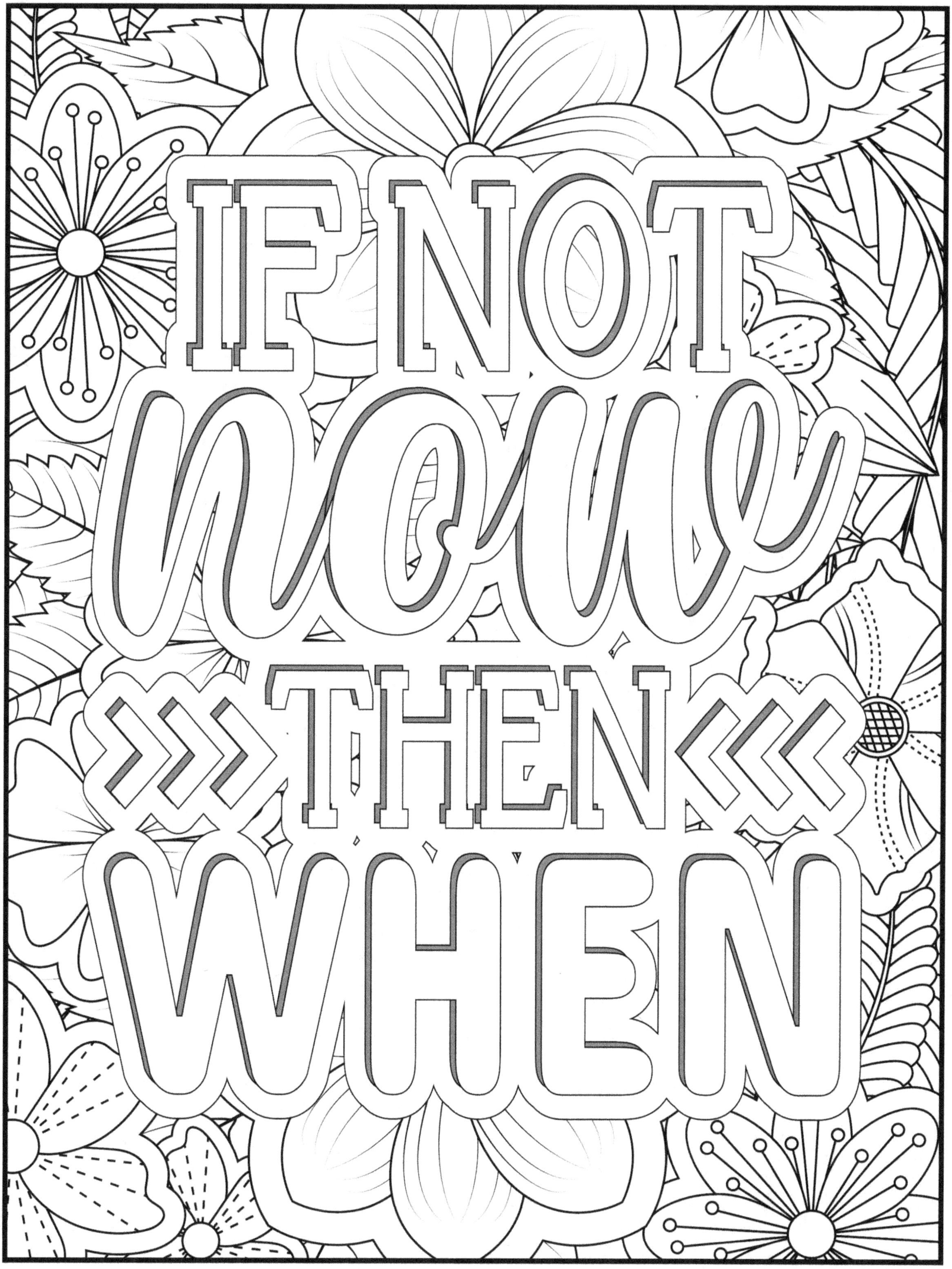
IF NOT
now
THEN
WHEN

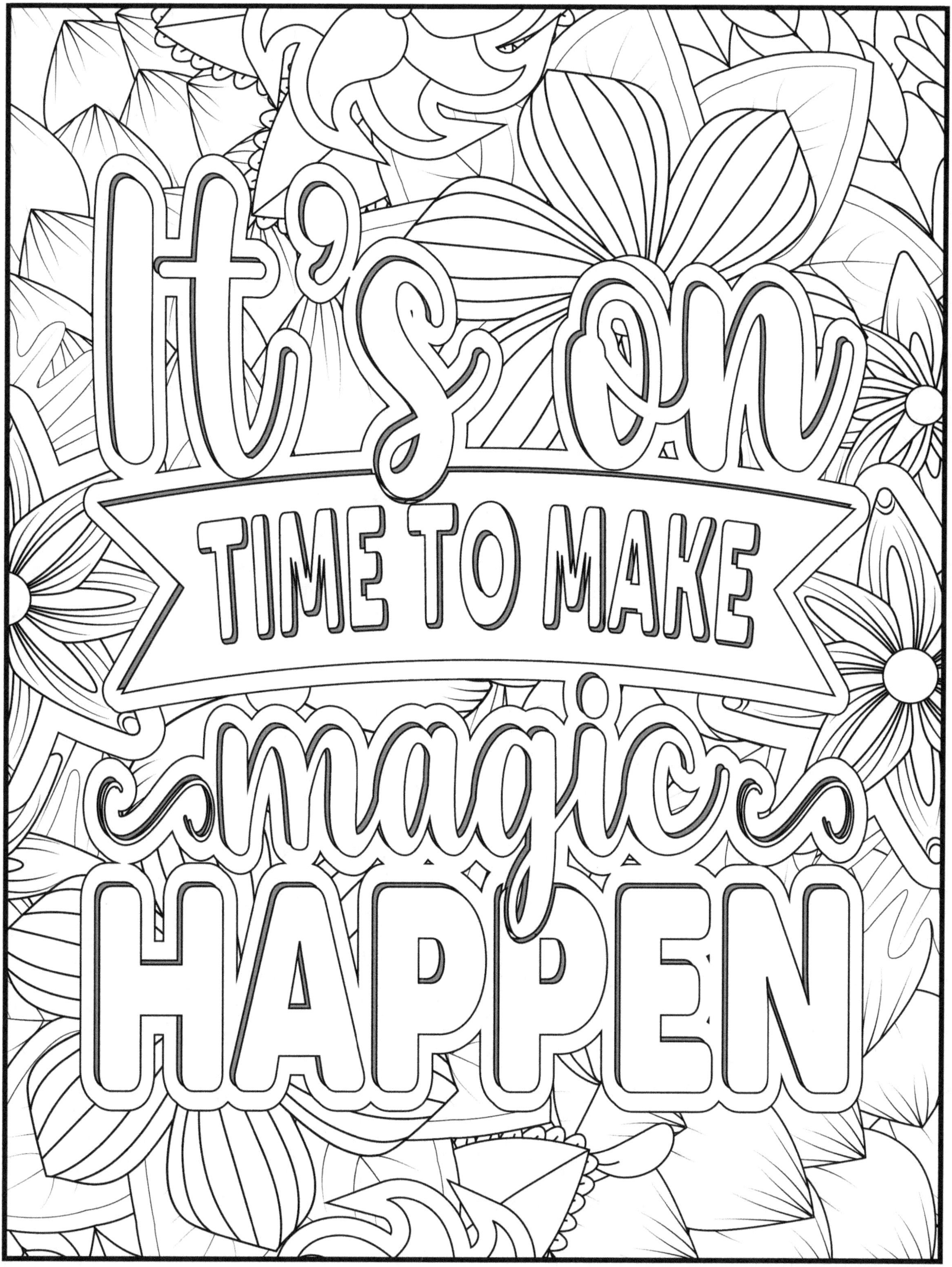

It's on
TIME TO MAKE
magic
HAPPEN

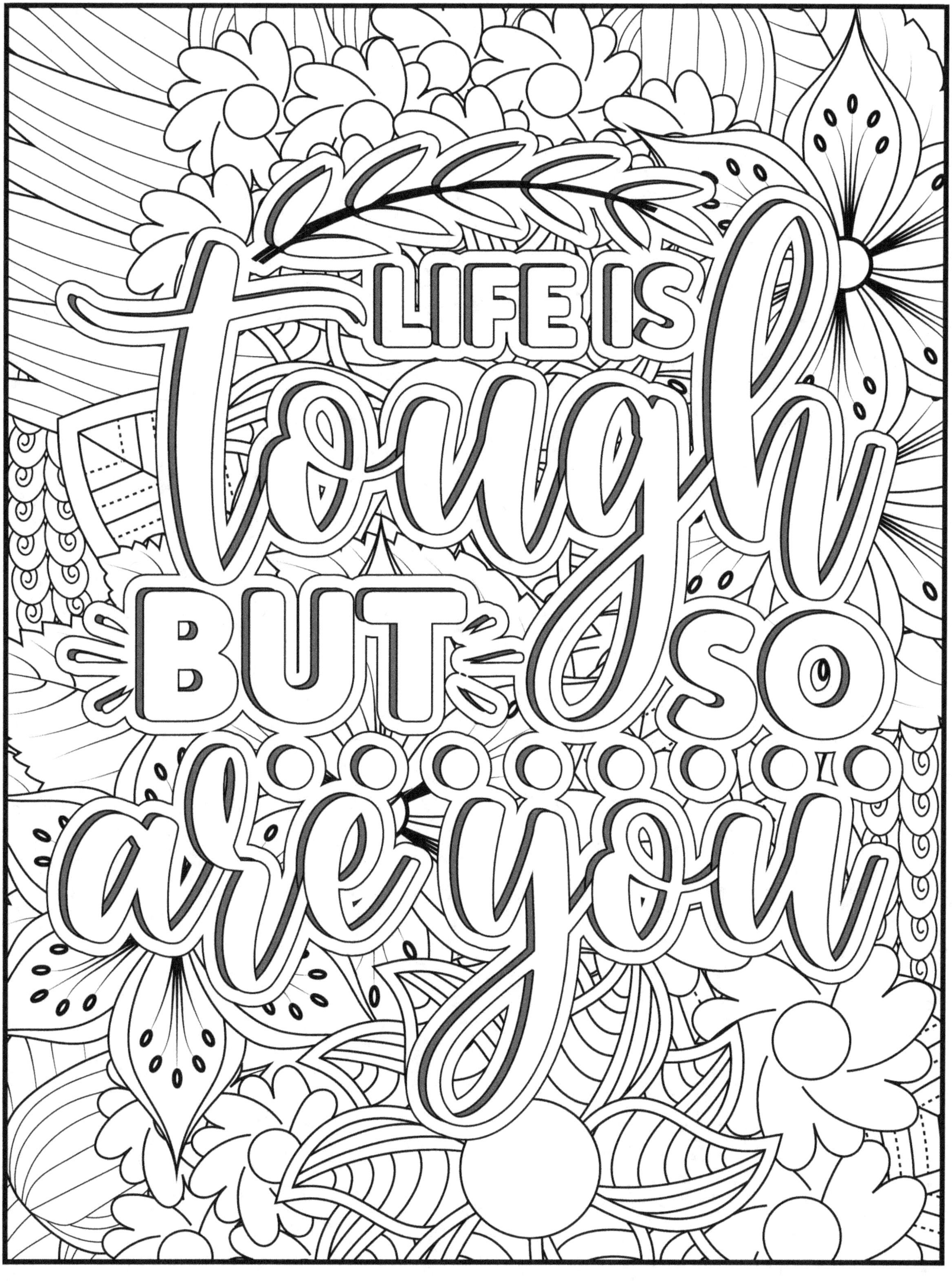
LIFE IS
tough
BUT SO
are you

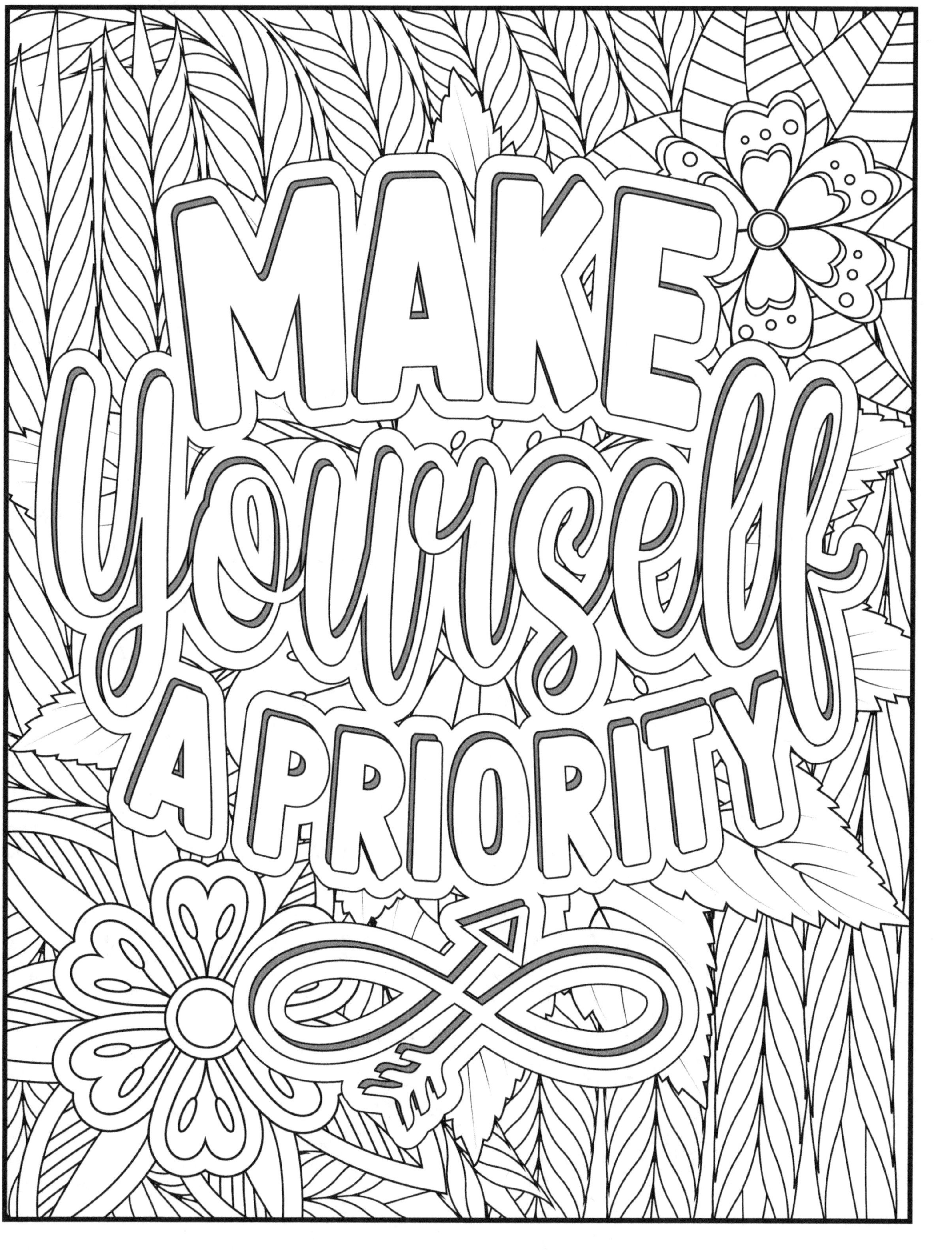
MAKE
yourself
A PRIORITY

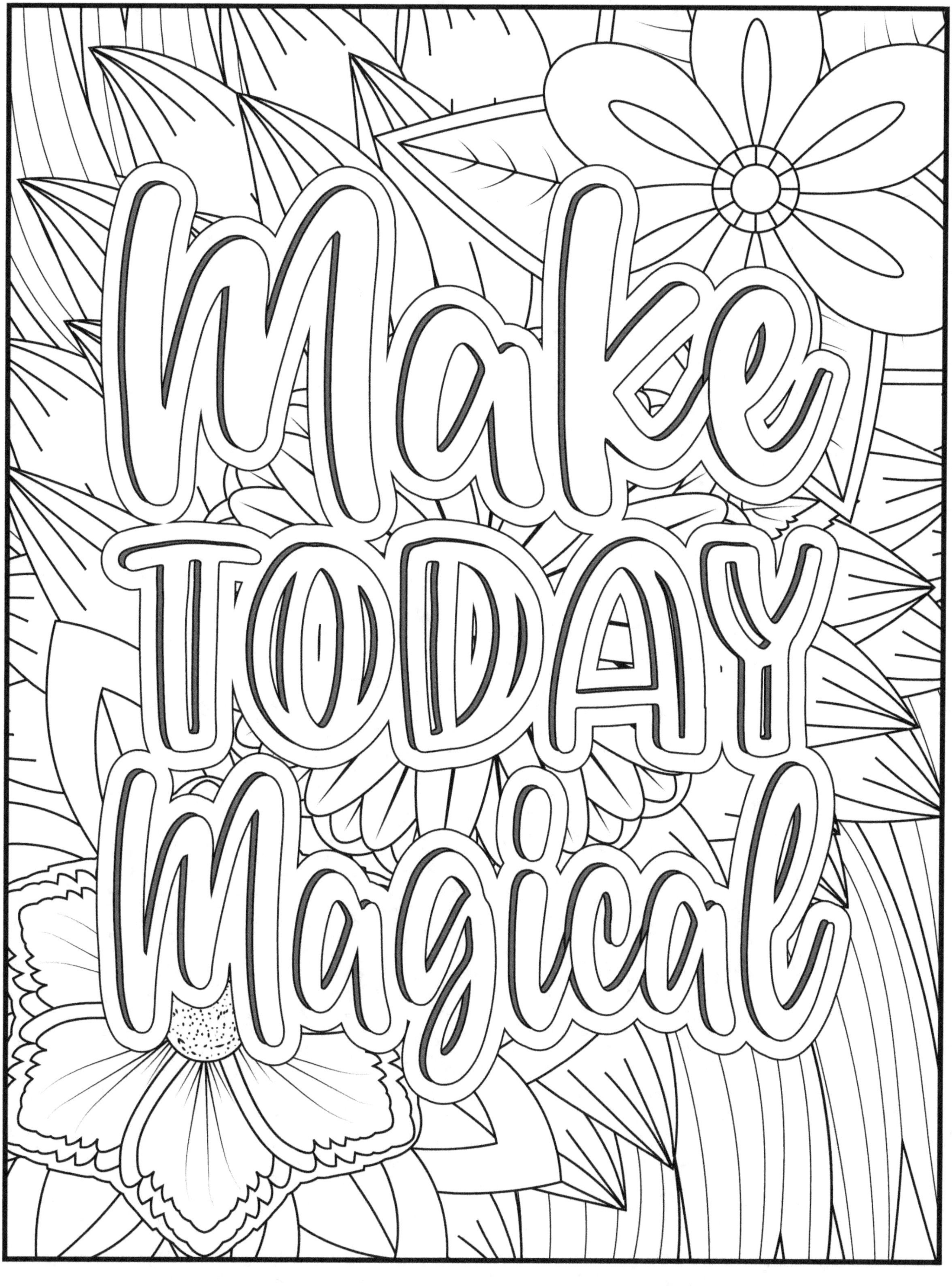
Make
TODAY
Magical

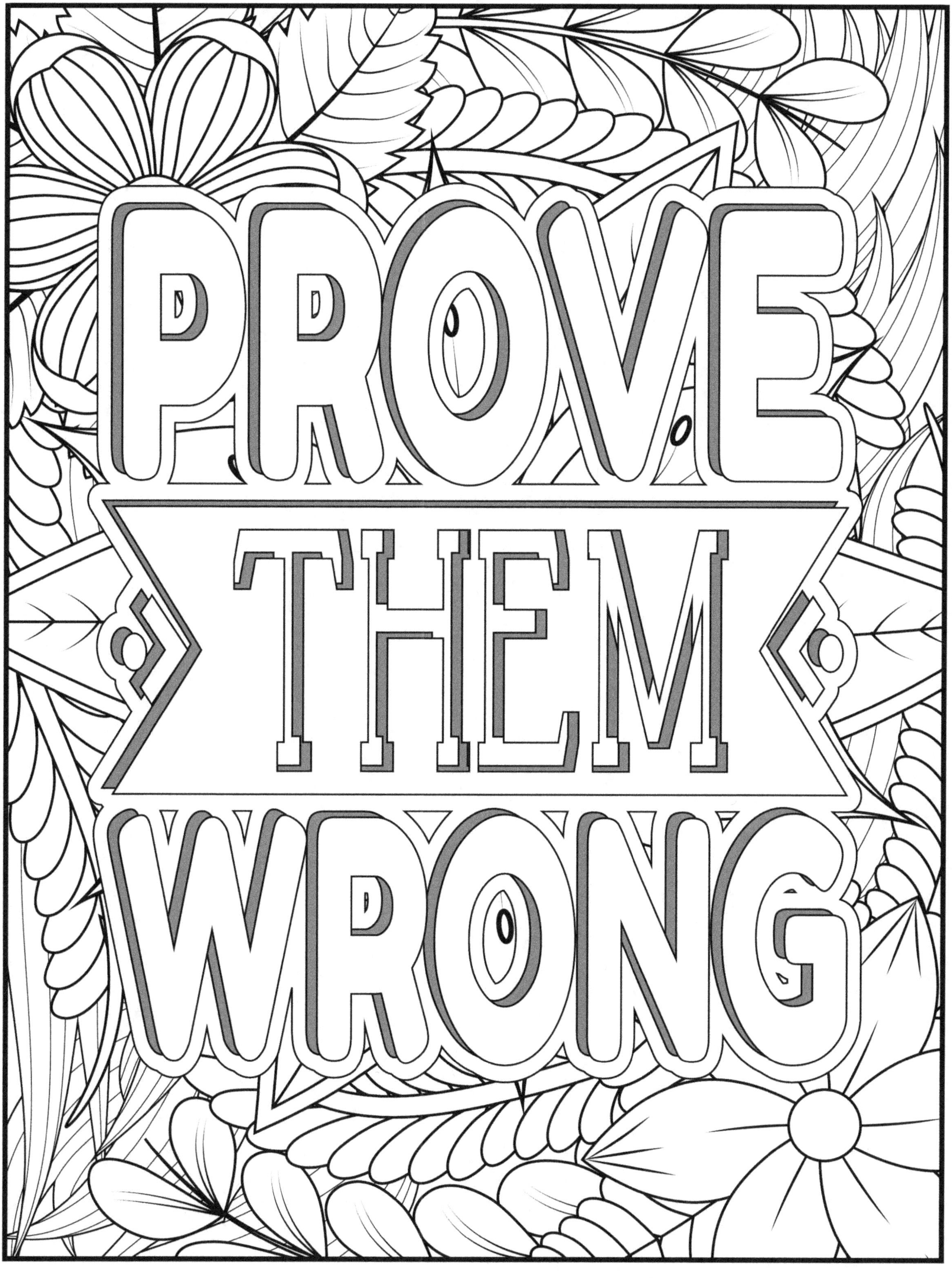
PROVE
THEM
WRONG

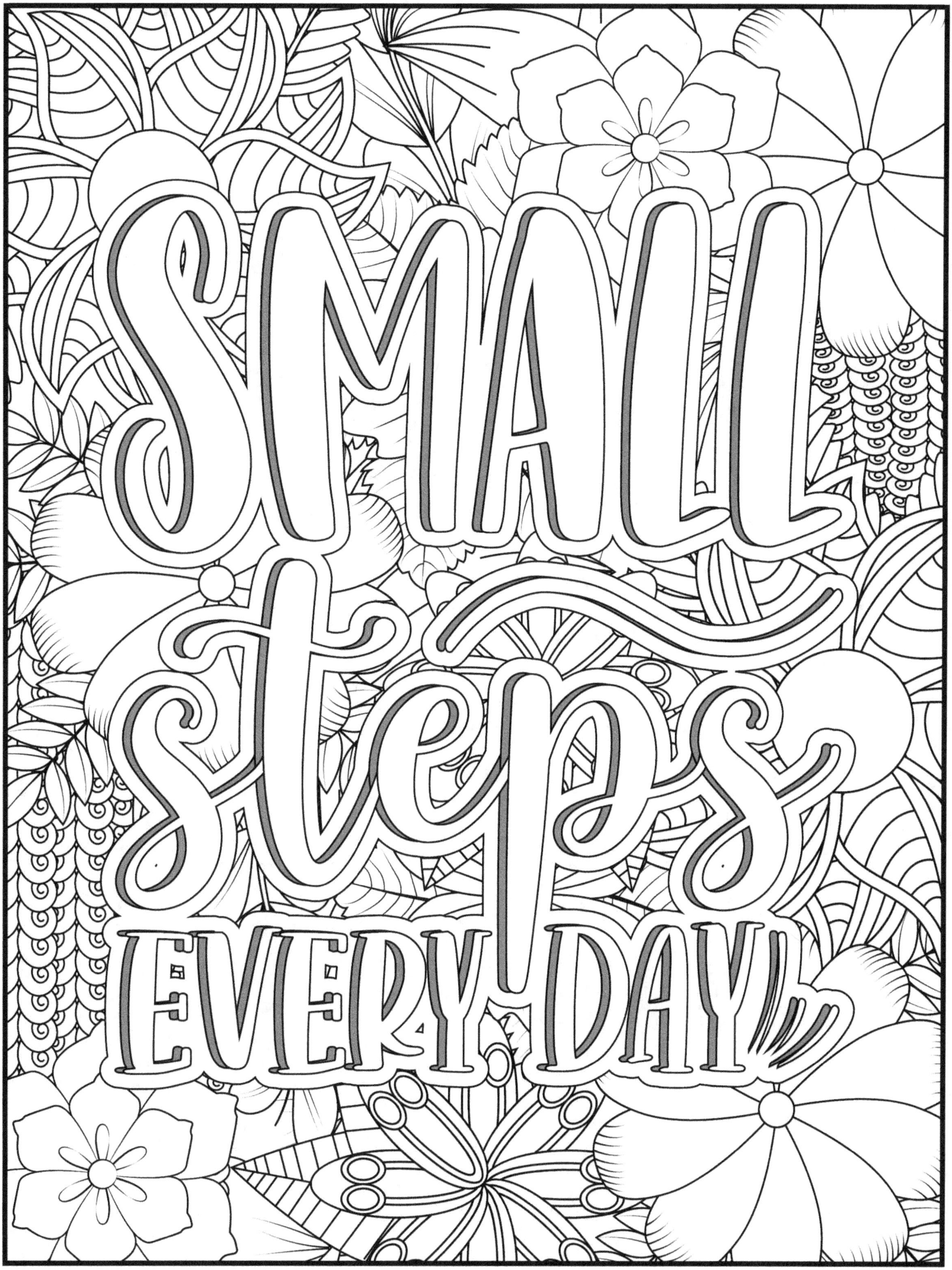
SMALL
steps
EVERY DAY

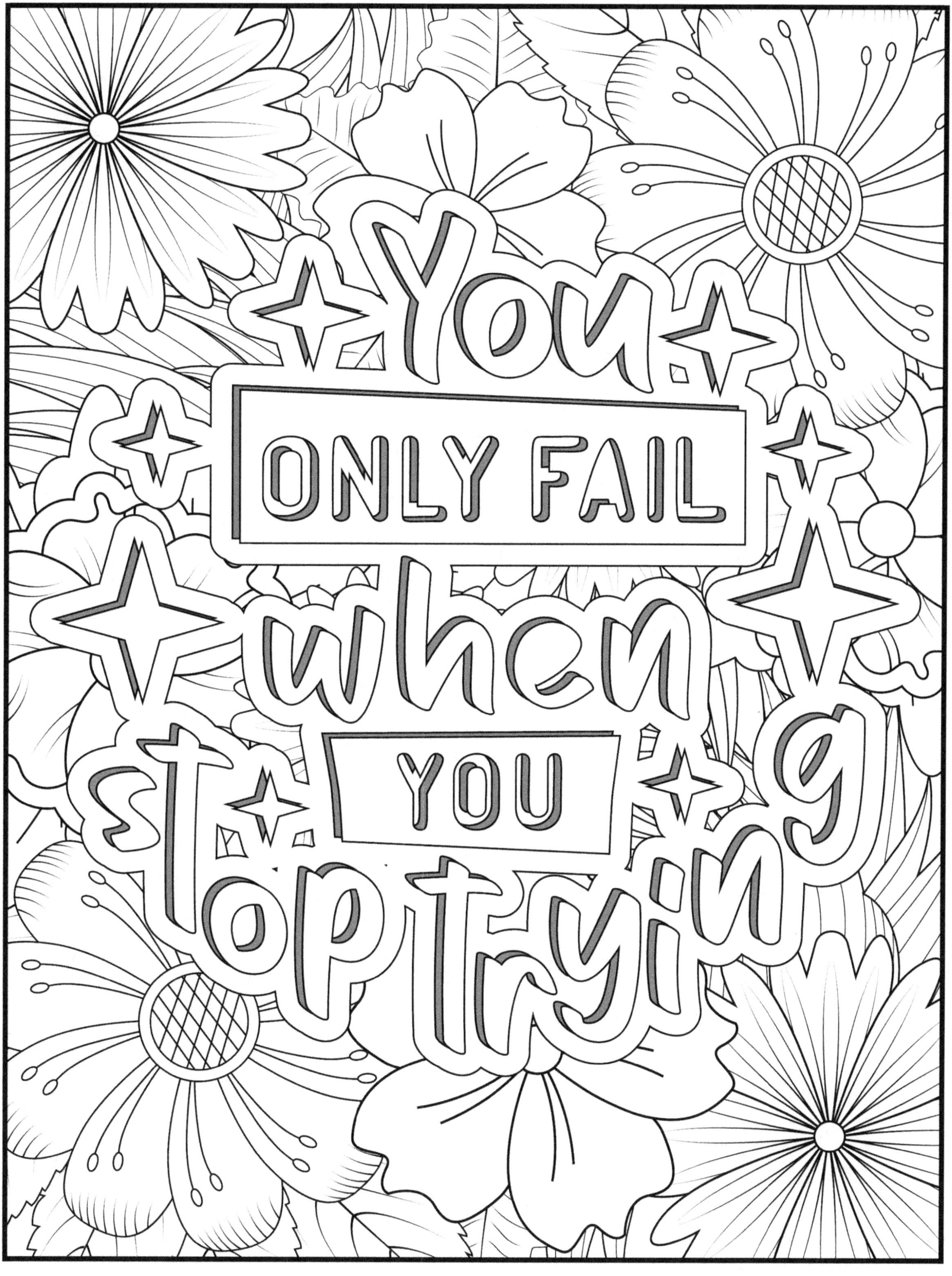
You
ONLY FAIL
when
YOU
stop trying

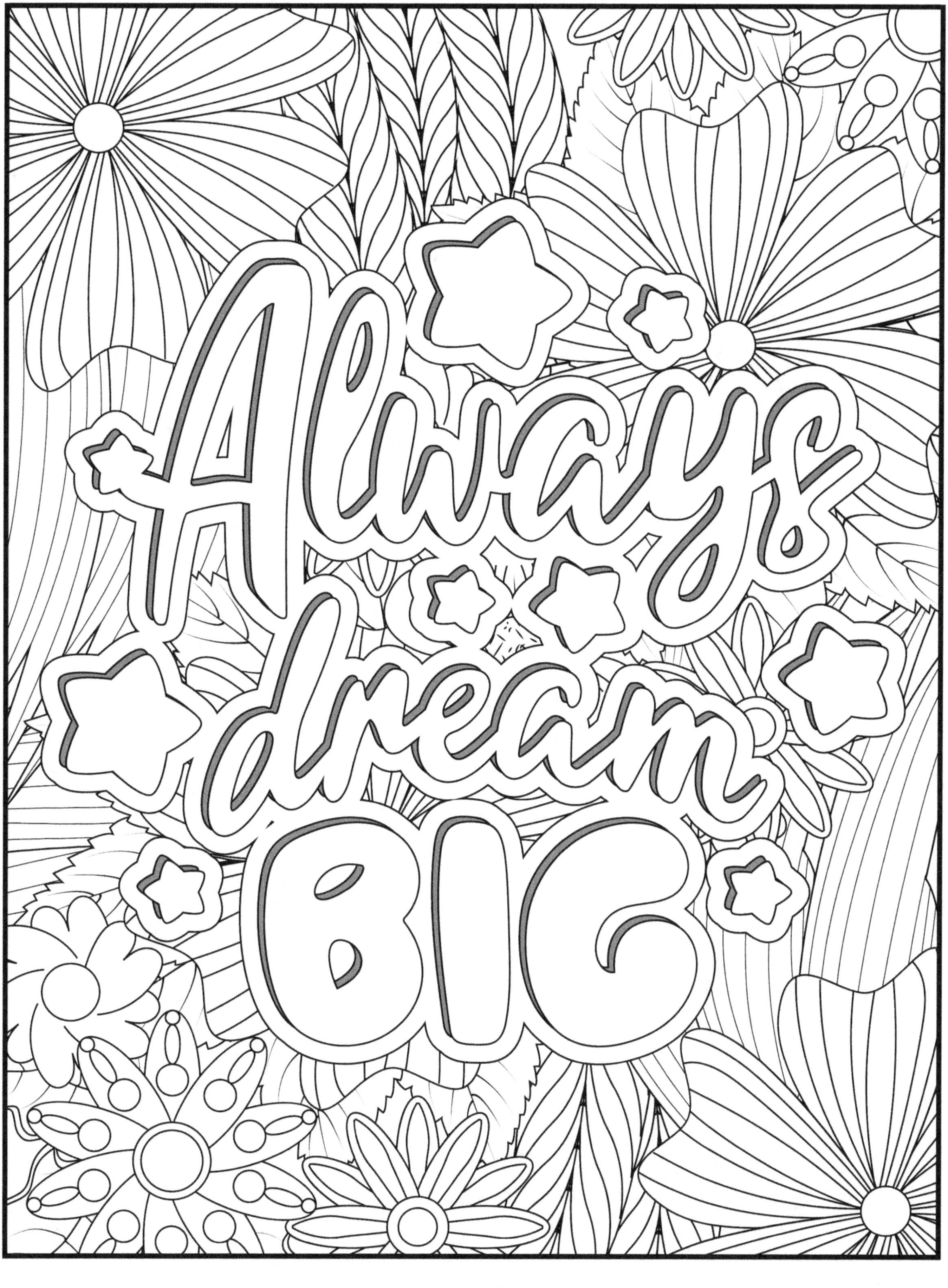
Always dream BIG

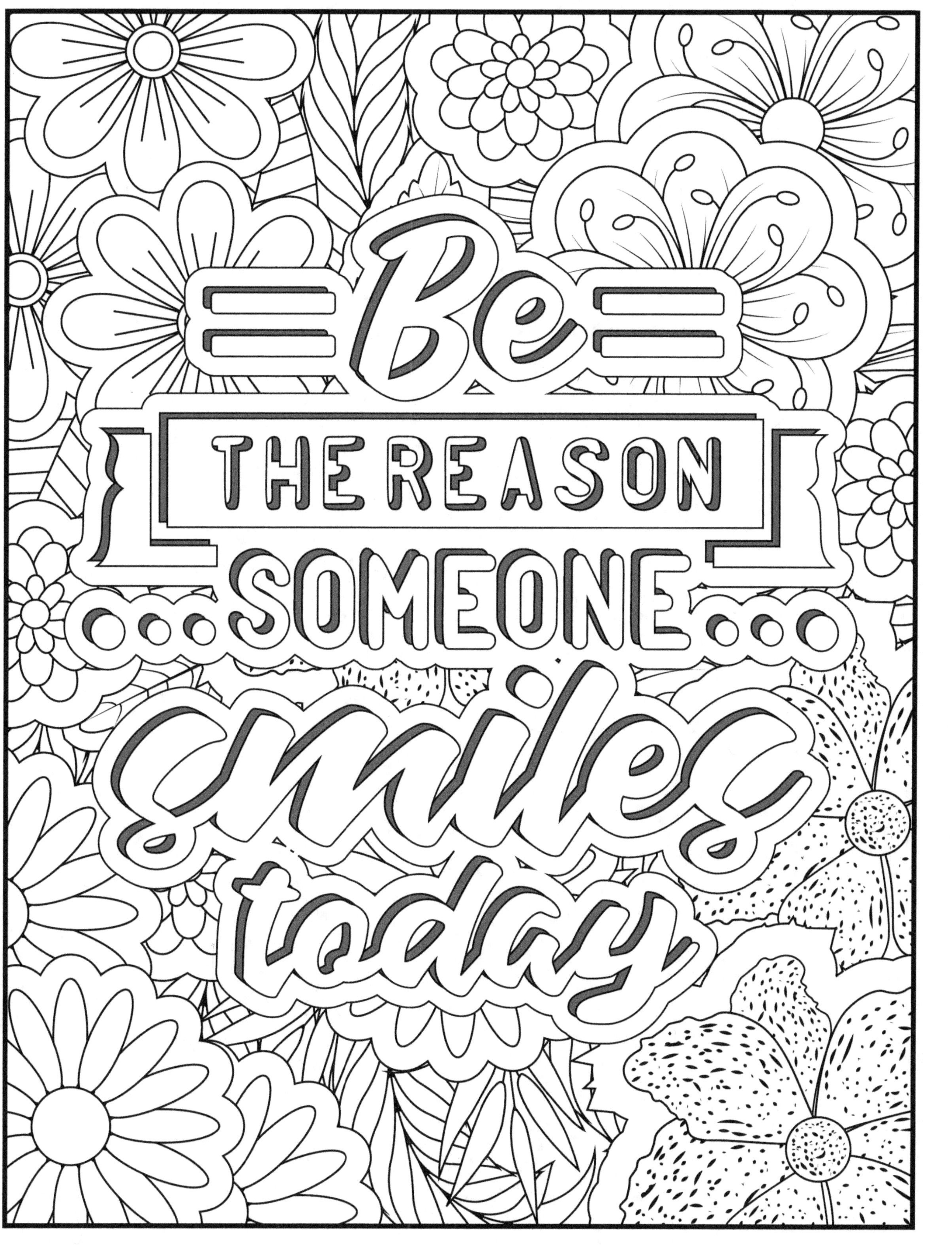
Be
THE REASON
SOMEONE
smiles
today

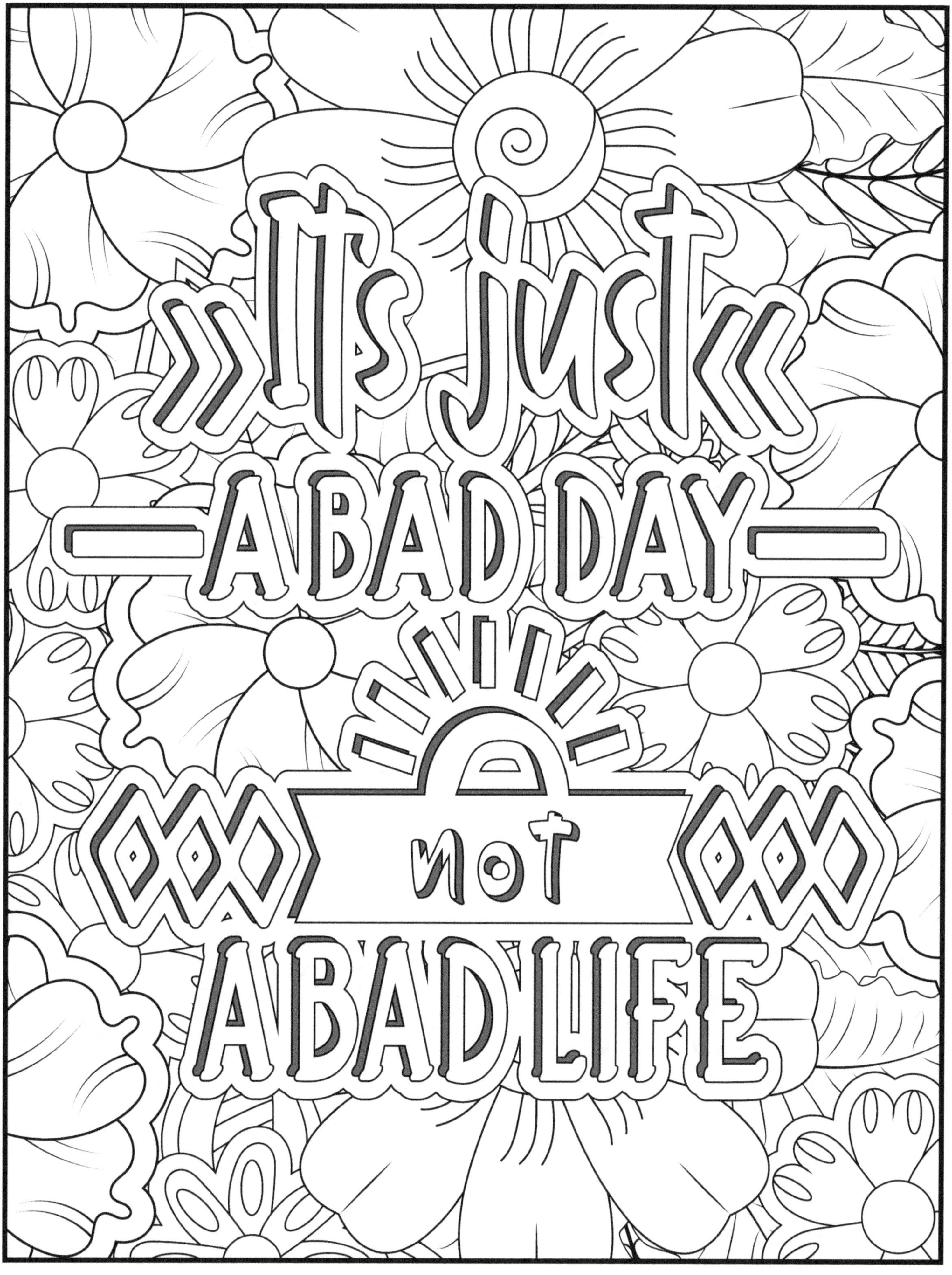
It's just
A BAD DAY
not
A BAD LIFE

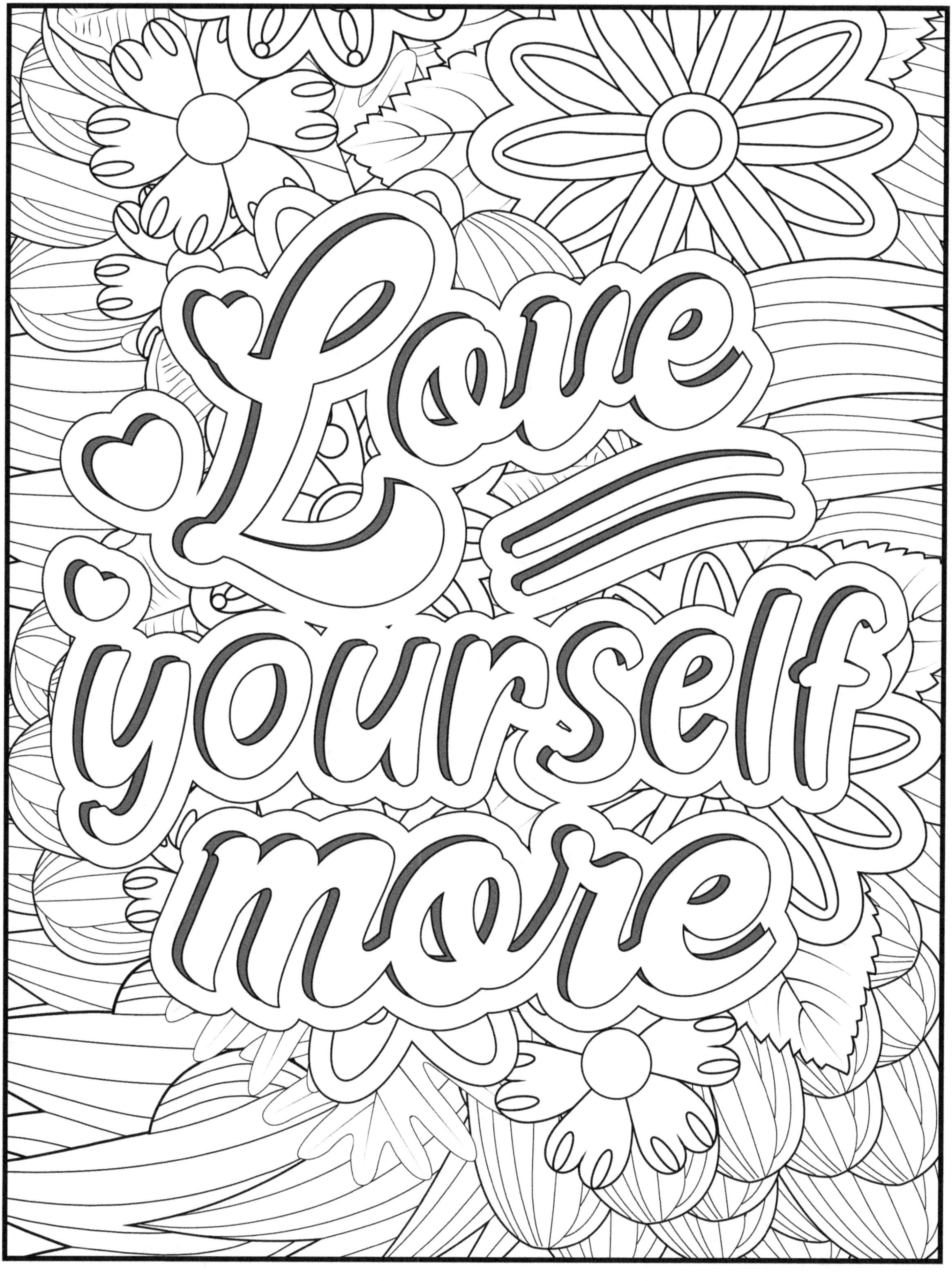
Love yourself more

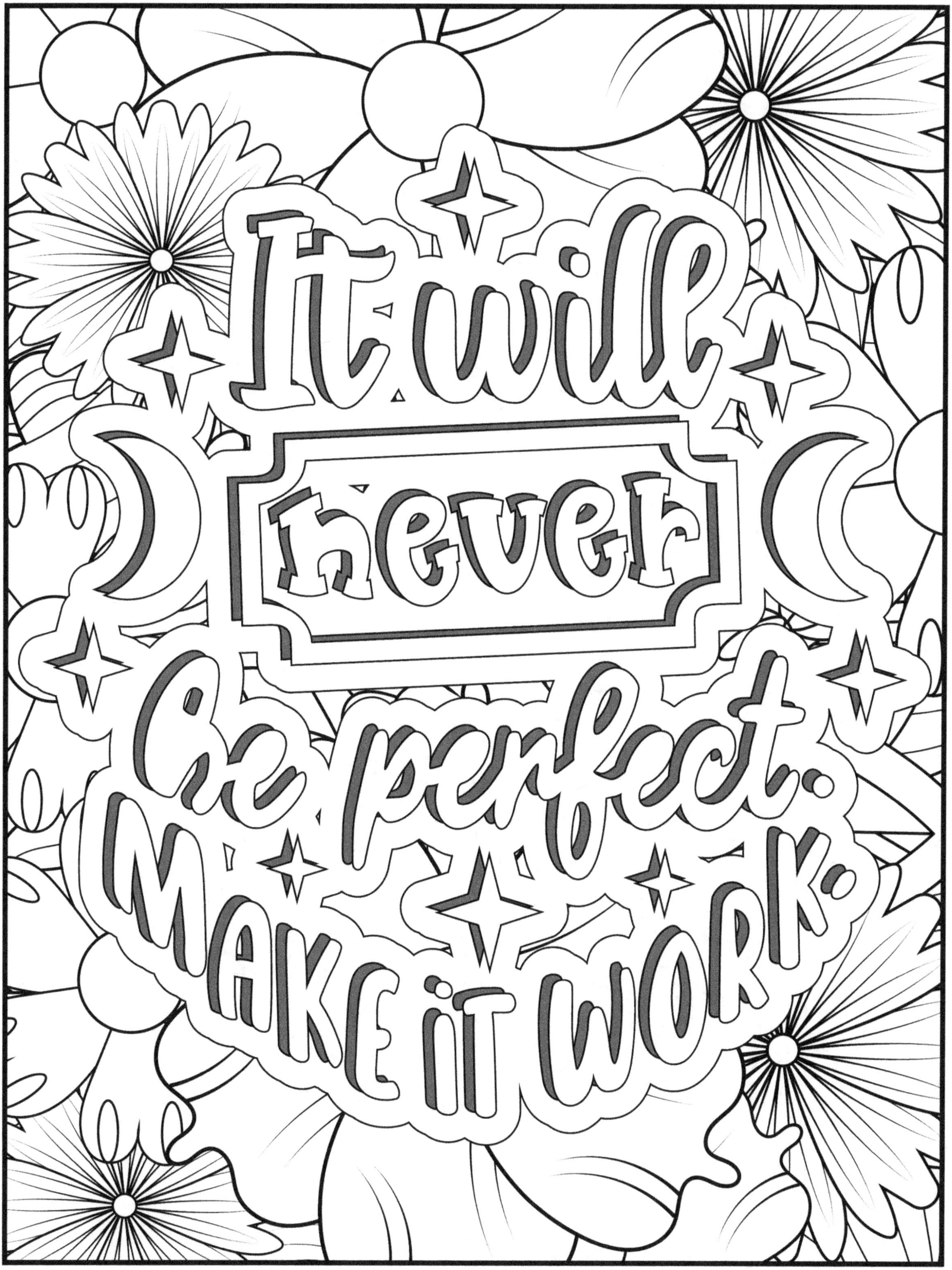
It will
never
be perfect.
MAKE IT WORK.

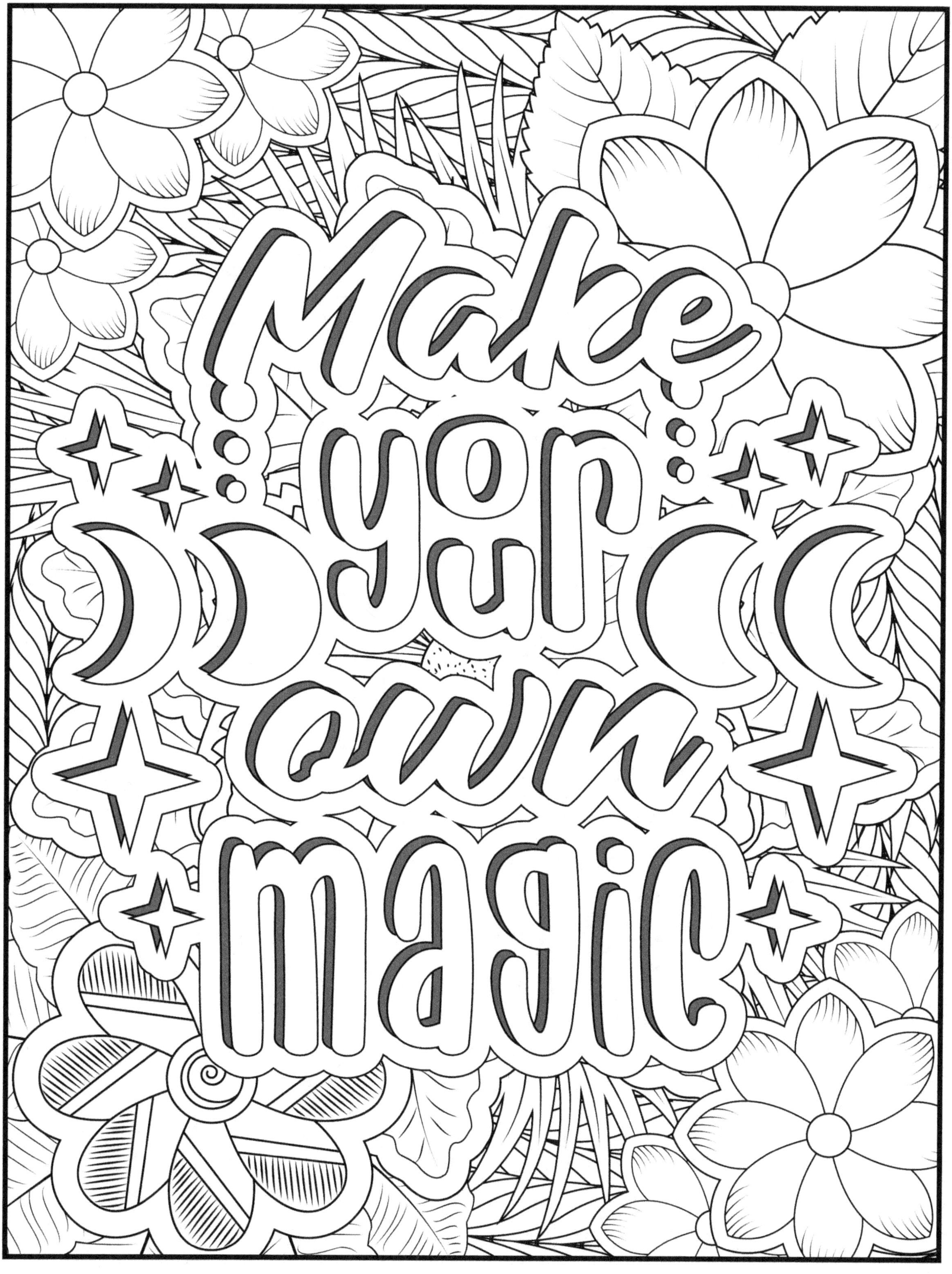
Make
your
own
magic

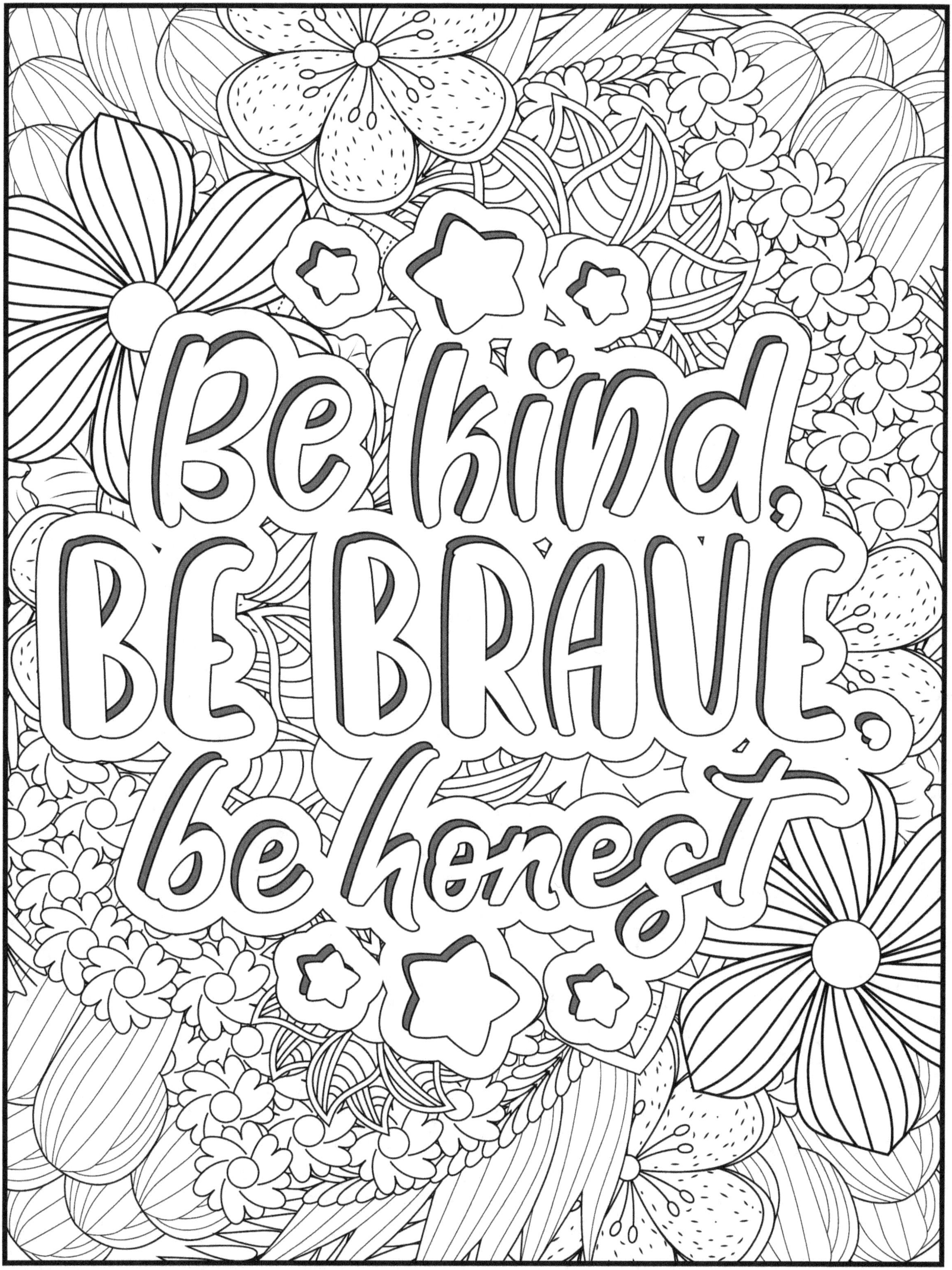
Be kind,
BE BRAVE,
be honest

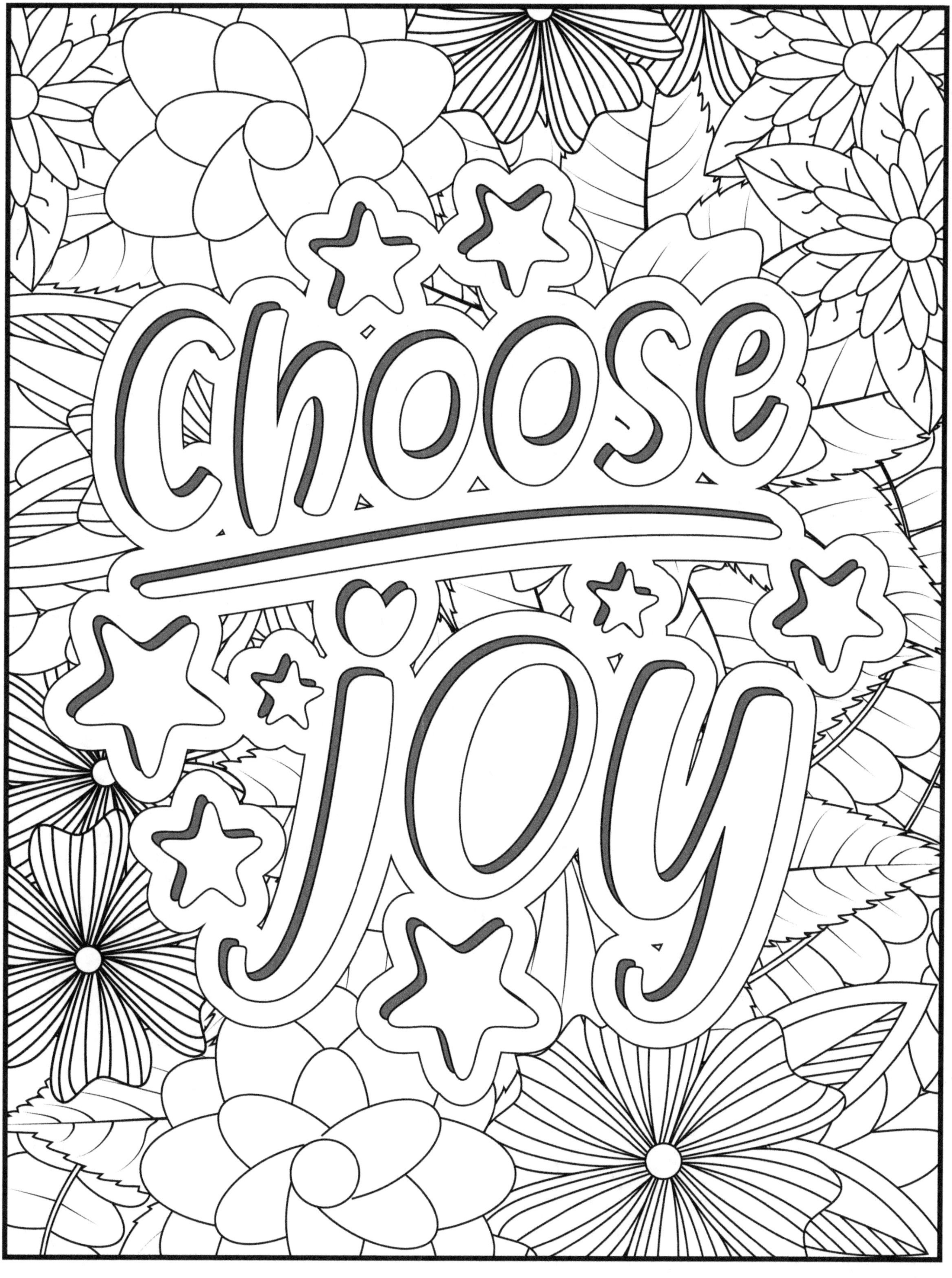
Choose
joy

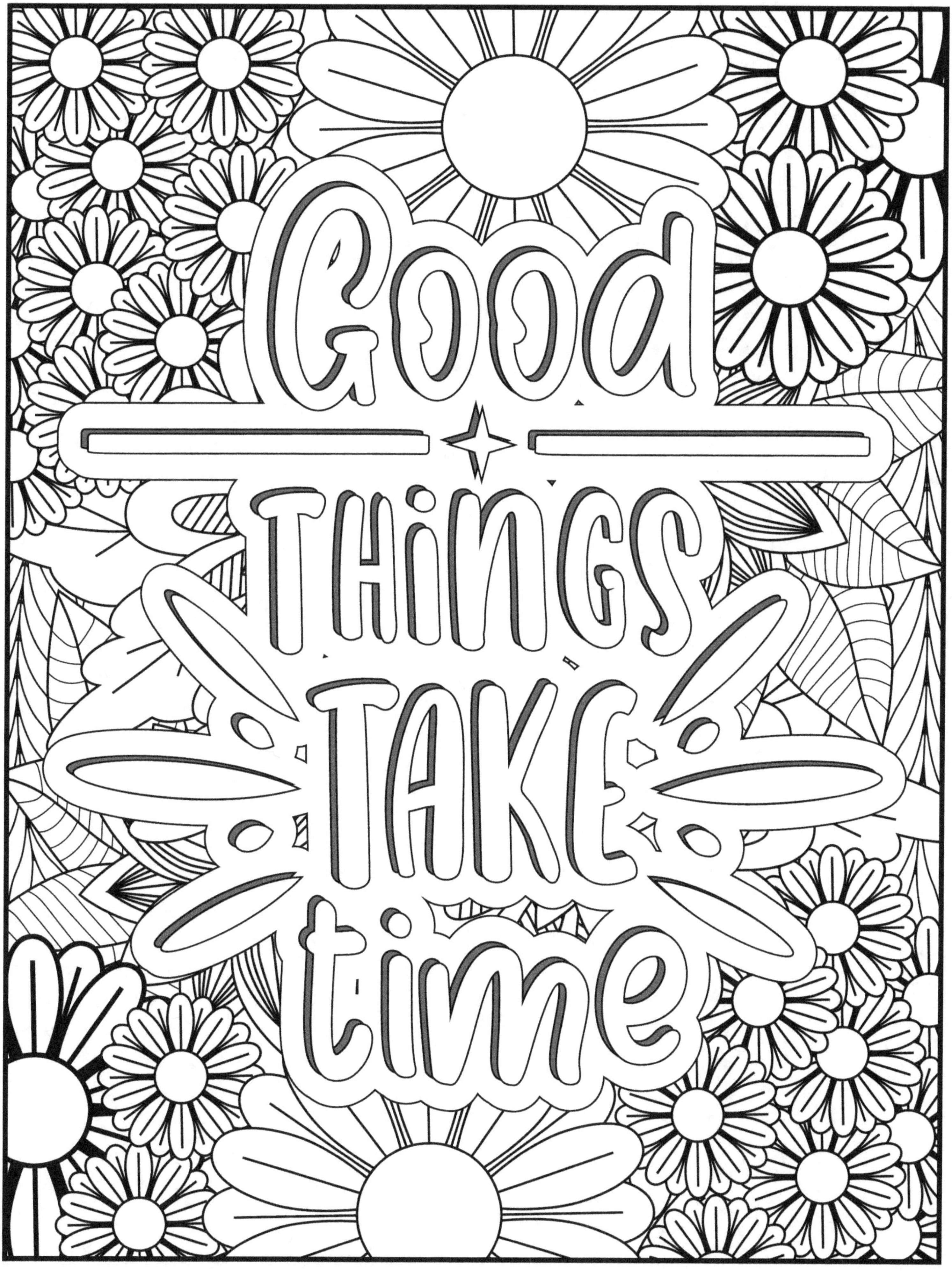
Good
THINGS
TAKE
time

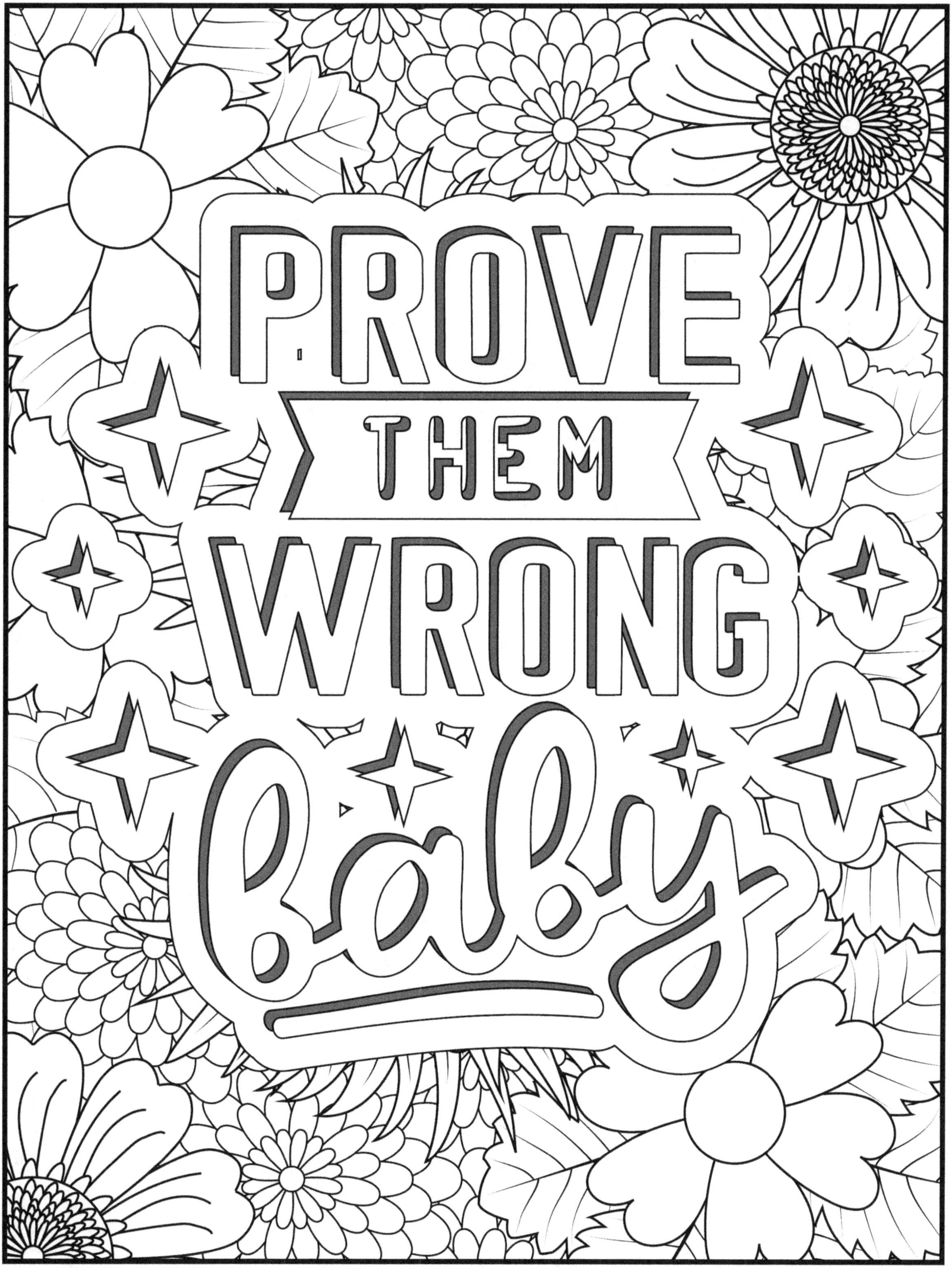
PROVE
THEM
WRONG
baby

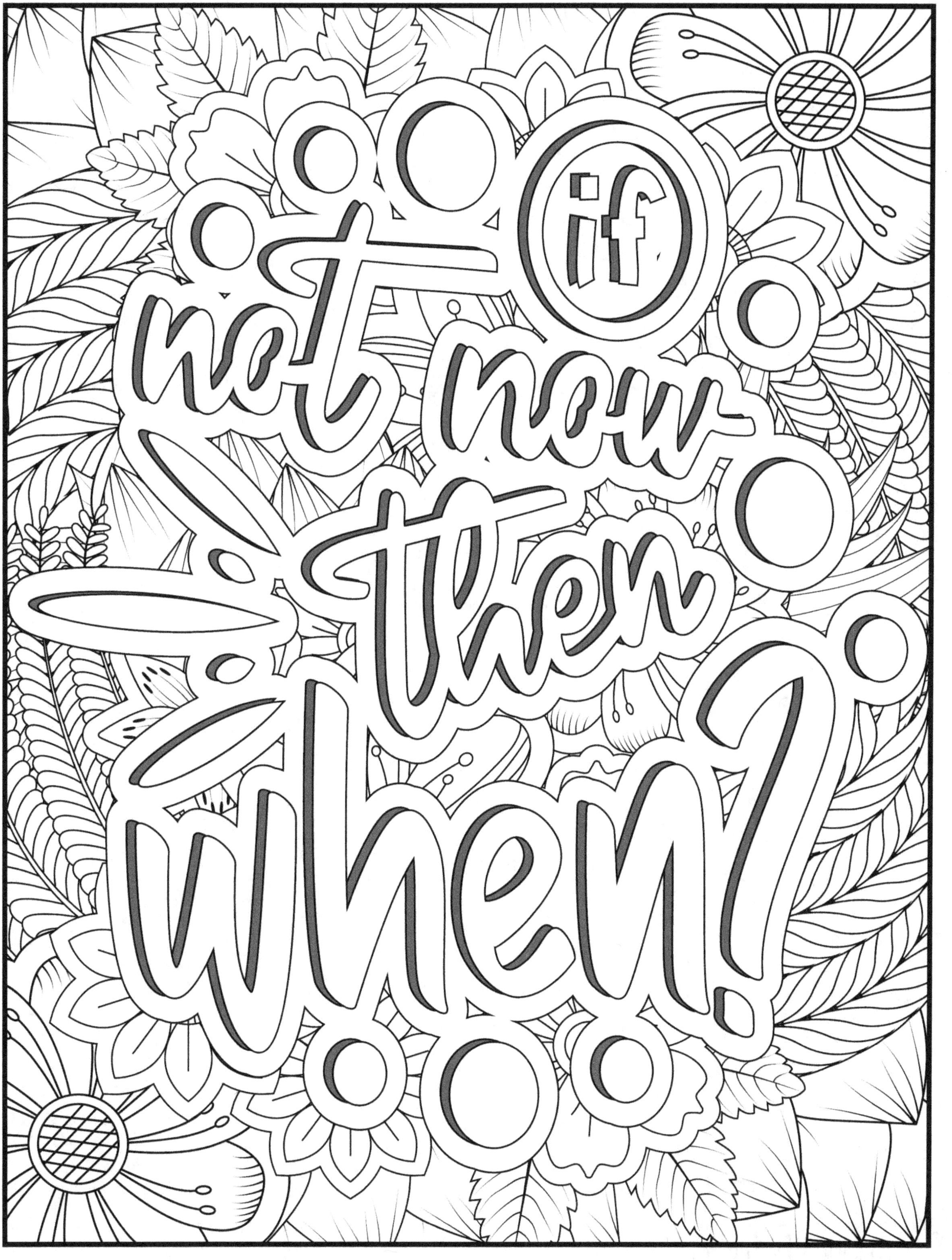
if
not now
then
when?

www.ingramcontent.com/pod-product-compliance
Lightning Source LLC
Chambersburg PA
CBHW082113220526
45472CB00009B/2161
9798328018623